The Determined Angler

and the

Brook Trout

An Anthological Volume of Trout Fishing,
Trout Histories, Trout Lore, Trout
Resorts, and Trout Tackle

By

Charles Bradford

To

J. CHARLES DAVIS

THESE LITTLE YARNS ARE DEDICATED IN REMEMBRANCE
OF SOME DELIGHTFUL OUTINGS PASSED
IN HIS SOCIETY.

THE BROOK TROUT'S HOME

"I am Salmo fontinalis.
To the sparkling fountain born;
And my home is where oxalis.
Heather bell and rose adorn
The crystal basin in the dell
(Undine the wood-nymph knows it well):
That is where I love to dwell.
There was I baptized and christened,
'Neath the somber aisles of oak;
Mute the cascade paused and listened.
Never a word the brooklet spoke;
Bobolink was witness then.
Likewise grosbeak, linnet, wren—
And all the fairies joined "amen!"
Thus as Salmo fontinalis
Recognized the wide world o'er.
In my limpid crystal palace.
Content withal, I ask no more.
Leaping through the rainbow spray.
Snatching flies the livelong day.
Naught to do but eat and play."
Charles Hallock.

BROOK TROUT ANGLING

"... it carries us into the most wild and beautiful scenery of nature; amongst the mountain lakes, and the clear and lovely streams that gush from the higher ranges of elevated hills, or that make their way through the cavities of calcareous strata. How delightful in the early spring, after the dull and tedious time of winter, when the frosts disappear and the sunshine warms the earth and waters, to wander forth by some clear stream, to see the leaf bursting from the purple bud, to scent the odors of the bank perfumed by the violet, and enameled, as it were, with the primrose and the daisy; to wander upon the fresh turf below the shade of trees, whose bright blossoms are filled with the music of the bee; and on the surface of the waters to view the gaudy flies sparkling like animated gems in the sunbeams, whilst the bright and beautiful trout is watching them from below; to hear the twittering of the water-birds, who, alarmed at your approach, rapidly hide themselves beneath the flowers and leaves of the water-lily; and as the season advances, to find all these objects changed for others of the same kind, but better and brighter, till the swallow and the trout contend as it were for the gaudy May fly, and till in pursuing your amusement in the calm and balmy evening, you are serenaded by the songs of the cheerful thrush ... performing the offices of paternal love, in thickets ornamented with the rose and woodbine."— Days of Fly Fishing, 1828.

viii

"Gentlemen, let not prejudice prepossess you. I confess my discourse is like to prove suitable to my recreation, calm and quiet.... And so much for the prologue of what I mean to say-"

Walton sig

PREFACE

"Don't give up if you don't catch fish; the unsuccessful trip should whet your appetite to try again."—Grover Cleveland.

A preface is either an excuse or an explanation, or both. The Brook Trout needs no excuse, and it is fully explained in the general text of this volume. Nor does the Angler, be he Determined or otherwise, need any excuse, because "our Saviour chose simple fishermen ... St. Peter, St. John, St. Andrew, and St. James, whom he inspired, and He never reproved these for their employment or calling" (Izaak Walton, The Compleat Angler, 1653). And the Angler—the man—needs no explanation, though it seems ever necessary to define the word.

Webster, himself a profound Angler, must have been unconscious of his gentle bearing, for his definition of "angle" is simply: "to fish," and every Angler knows that merely to fish—to go forth indifferent of correct (humane) tackle, the legal season, and ethical methods in the pursuit—is not the way of the Angler.

I like the explanation of the word by Genio C. Scott: "Angling, a special kind of fishing."

2

The inspired landscape genius and the kalsominer who shellacs the artist's studio are both painters; so, the gentle Angler with perfect tackle and the mere hand-line fish taker are both fishermen.

The Angler is the highest order of fisherman, x and while all Anglers are fishermen there are many fishermen who are not Anglers.

"Anglo-Saxon," writing in the New York Press. October 14, 1915, uses the term "gentleman Anglers." He should have said "gentleman fishermen" (Anglers), because all Anglers are gentlemen, regardless of their business calling, appearance, personality, companionship, etc. When a man, fisherman or no fisherman, develops into an Angler he must first become gentle in order to be of the gentle art. "Angling is the gentle art" (Walton). "The gentle art of angling" (Cotton).

"If true Anglers," says Genio C. Scott, "you are sure to be gentle."

Peter Flint (New York Press, Oct. 15, 1915): "Our most successful Anglers, amateurs as well as professionals."

All Anglers are amateurs, brother Peter. There are no professional Anglers, though there are both amateur and professional fishermen, and those fishermen who are amateurs are Anglers. The word "amateur" seems to be adrift upon the same bewildering tideway as the words "angler" and "angling." "Amateur" hasn't the definition commonly attributed to it—it doesn't signify inefficiency, inexperience, unpracticality, etc., as do the words "beginner," "neophyte," "tyro," etc. An amateur in fishing, or farming, or any other pastime or pursuit, may be far more practical, more experienced, more proficient, and better equipped in tools and paraphernalia than a professional, and he usually is so; he is certainly always so in angling.

Watch your word.

"It is the belief of Acker that hand-line fishing is as xi good [as, if not better than, the rod and reel kind." (Wandering Angler, New York Press, Aug. 17, 1915.)

Hand-line fishing, as fishing,—though the Tuna Angling Club, of Santa Catalina Island, California, is bound to the use of light rods and fine reels and tells us hand-lines are unsportsmanlike and detrimental to the public interest,—is good (Christ and His disciples sanctioned it), but to say it is as good as or better than rod and reel angling is not convincing. The indifferent fisher can't condemn angling in praising common fishing with any more reason than he might proclaim against cricket playing in favoring carpentry, or vice versa. One might as correctly say hand-line fishing is as good as riding, or driving, or golf, or baseball, or canoeing (of course it is), for fishing without rod and reel and fishing with proper tackle are pursuits as distinct in character as riding a plain horse bareback with a rough halter, and straddling a gallant charger with neat bridle and saddle; or as mere boating upon a refuse creek, and skimming the green billows in a trim yacht.

That the fisher's hand-line and the fisherman's net will take more fish than the Angler's tackle is not of moment, because a stick of dynamite or a cannon filled with leaden pellets or a boy with a market basket will take still more fish than the net and

3

hand-line. Quantity makes fishing "good" with the fisherman; quality delights the Angler. There is no objection to the mere fish-getter filling his boat with fishes with or without tackle, but as the jockey is separated from the sportsman rider and the sailor from the yachtsman so should the quantity fisher and the quality Angler be considered in contrasting spheres. "What a man brings home in his heart after fishing xii is of more account than what he brings in his basket," says W. J. Long. "Anglers encourage the adoption of angling methods," says Dr. Van Dyke, "which make the wholesale slaughter of fishes impossible and increase the sport of taking a fair number in a fair way."

As chivalric single-missile bow-and-arrow exercise dignifies archery above bunch-arrow work in war, so the gentle use of refined tackle dignifies angling above mere fish getting. Trap shooting is delightful, and more birds are killed than the gunner would bag in marsh and meadow, but is trap shooting therefore more "good" than game-shooting in the glorious fields and forests? No, sir; and though the hand-line fisherman may honestly take half the ocean's yield, still his pursuit and his catch cannot equal and cannot be legitimately compared to the code and the creel of the competent Angler.

C. B.

Richmond Hill,
Long Island, n. y.,
March, 1916.

xiii

AUTHOR'S ACKNOWLEDGMENTS

The article "Fly Fishing for Trout," I contributed in its original form to Sports Afield, Mr. Claude King's Western journal.

The article "Trout and Trouting," as I originally prepared it, was entitled "Near-by Trout Streams," and was written for and published in Outing, when I was field editor of that delightful magazine.

"Trouting in Canadensis Valley" is rewritten from a little story of mine penned at the suggestion of the noted angler and ichthyologist, the late William C. Harris, and published by him in his The American Angler when I became his managing editor.

"Trout Flies, Artificial and Natural" and "The Brook Trout Incognito" are elaborations of studies I composed for Forest and Stream.

And many of the items in "Little Casts," etc., are from a collection of paragraphs I have contributed to the New York Herald, the New York Press, and various sporting periodicals in past years.

The extracts from the article by Willis Boyd Allen are reprinted by permission of Scribner's Magazine.

4

For the little pen-and-ink sketches I am indebted to our jovial artist, Leppert.

CHAPTER I

THE HOLY ANGLERS

"The greater number of them [Christ's disciples were found together, fishing, by Jesus, after His Resurrection."—Izaak Walton.

"... certain poor fishermen coming in very weary after a night of toil (and one of them very wet after swimming ashore) found their Master standing on the bank of the lake waiting for them. But it seems that He must have been busy in their behalf while he was waiting; for there was a bright fire of coals on the shore, and a goodly fish broiling thereon, and bread to eat with it. And when the Master had asked them about their fishing he said: 'Come, now, and get your breakfast.' So they sat down around the fire, and with His own hands he served them with the bread and the fish."—Henry Van Dyke.

"The first men that our Saviour dear
Did choose to wait upon Him here.
Blest fishers were...."
—W. Basse
"I would ... fish in the sky whose bottom is pebbly with stars."—Thoreau.

The principal fishes of the Sea of Galilee to-day are the same as they were two thousand years ago—bream 2 and chub. These were taken in olden times by both net and hook and line.

The fishermen whom Christ chose as His disciples—Peter. Andrew, James, and John—were professional net fishermen, but hook and line fishing was a favorite pastime of the well-to-do Egyptians as well as the poor people who could not afford a net.

Weirs not unlike the modern article were used in the Holy Land in Bible time, excepting on Lake Gennesaret, where the law of the land forbade them.

The bream and the chub were eaten alike by rich and poor people. Wayfarers roasted them over chip fires in the groves and on the lake shores, housewives boiled and broiled them, and the wealthy man served them at his banquets. "Moses, the friend of God," writes Izaak Walton, in his immortal Compleat Angler, quoting from Lev. xi., 9, Deut., xiv., 9, "appointed fish to be the chief diet for the best commonwealth that ever yet was. The mightiest feasts have been of fish."

Our Saviour "fed the people on fish when they were hungry." The species is not alluded to in the Biblical paragraph, but no doubt the fish feasts of the Lord were mostly of chub and bream. Jesus loved fishermen and was in their society most of His time. No other class of men were so well favored by Him. He inspired St. Peter, St. John, St. Andrew, and St. James, poor fishermen, who drew their nets for the people, and these four fishermen, declares Father Izaak, "He never reproved for their employment or calling, as he did scribes and money changers."

The Lord's favorite places of labor and repose—the places He most frequented—were near the fishes and fisherman. "He began to teach by the seaside. 3 His pulpit was a fishing boat or the shore of a lake. He was in the stern of the boat, asleep. He was always near the water to cheer and comfort those who followed it." And Walton tells us that "when God intended to reveal high notions to His prophets He carried them to the shore, that He might settle their mind in a quiet repose."

Bream and chub are not monster fishes—they do not average the great weights of the tarpon and the tuna; they are of the small and medium-size species; so, if the apostles were pleased with "ye gods and little fishes," we mortals of to-day should be satisfied with our catch, be it ever so small.

APPELLATIONS OF THE TROUTS

Trout, Bear: See Lake Trout
Trout, Beardslee: See Crescent Lake Blue-Back
Trout, Black-spotted Salmon
Trout, Blue-Back: See Oquassa Trout
Trout, Brook
Trout, Brown
Trout, Canada: See Greenland Trout
Trout, Canada Sea: See Brook Trout and Greenland Trout
Trout, Colorado River: See Black-Spotted
Trout, Columbia River: See Black-Spotted
Trout, Cousin: See Roach
Trout, Crescent Lake Blue-Back
Trout, Crescent Lake Long-Headed
Trout, Crescent Lake Speckled
Trout, Dolly Varden: See Malma Trout
Trout, Dublin Pond
Trout, European Brown
Trout, Fresh-Water Cod: See Lake Trout
Trout, Golden: See Rainbow Salmon Trout and Sunapee
Trout, Great Lakes: See Mackinaw
Trout, Green: See Black Bass
Trout, Green-Back
Trout, Greenland
Trout, Hard-Head: See Steel-Head Salmon Trout
Trout, Jordan
Trout, Kansas River: See Kansas River Salmon Trout
Trout, Kern River: See Rainbow
Trout, Lac de Marbre
Trout, Lake
Trout, Lake Salmon: See Lake Trout
Trout, Lake Southerland Salmon

Trout, Lake Southerland Spotted: See Jordan's Trout

5 Trout, Lake Tahoe: See Lake Tahoe Salmon Trout

Trout, Lewis: See Yellowstone Trout

Trout, Loch Leven

Trout, Lunge: See Lake Trout

Trout, Mackinaw: See Mackinaw Lake Trout

Trout, Mackinaw Lake

Trout, Malma

Trout, Marston: See Lac de Marbre Trout

Trout, Mountain: See Brook Trout, Small-Mouth Black Bass, and Rainbow Salmon Trout

Trout, Mt. Whitney: See Rainbow

Trout, Mucqua Lake: See Lake Trout

Trout, Namaycush: See Lake Trout

Trout, Namaycush Lake

Trout, Nissuee: See Rainbow

Trout, Noshee: See Rainbow

Trout, Oquassa

Trout, Pickerel: See Long Island Pickerel

Trout, Pickerel: See Long Island Pickerel

Trout, Pike: See Long Island Pickerel

Trout, Pike: See Long Island Pickerel

Trout, Rainbow: See Rainbow Salmon Trout

Trout, Rainbow Lake: See Rainbow Salmon Trout

Trout, Red: See Lac de Marbre Trout

Trout, Red-Spotted: See Malma Trout

Trout, Rio Grande: See Rio Grande Salmon Trout

Trout, Rio Grande Salmon

Trout, Saibling

Trout, Salmon

Trout, Sea: See Greenland Trout and Brook Trout

Trout, Silver: See Black-Spotted Salmon Trout and Lake Tahoe Salmon Trout

Trout, Siskawitz: See Lake Trout

Trout, Siscowet: See Lake Trout

Trout, Stone's: See Rainbow

Trout, Sunapee

Trout, Tahoe

Trout, Togue: See Lake Trout

Trout, Truckee: See Lake Tahoe

Trout, Tuladi: See Lake Trout

Trout, Utah

6 Trout, Waha Lake: See Waha Lake Salmon Trout

Trout, Waha Lake Salmon

Trout, Western Oregon Brook: See Rainbow

Trout, White: See Sunapee

Trout, Winipiseogee: See Lake Trout

Trout, Yellow-Fin

Trout, Yellowstone

CHAPTER II

HISTORIES OF THE TROUTS—HOW THE ANGLER TAKES THEM

Trout, Brook (Speckled Trout, Mountain Trout. Fontinalis, Speckled Beauty, Spotted Trout, etc.): Caught in the spring and summer in clear streams, lakes, and ponds, on the artificial fly. Favors eddies, riffles, pools, and deep spots under the banks of the stream and near rocks and fallen trees. Feeds on small fish, flies, and worms. Breeds in the autumn. Weighs up to ten pounds in large waters. There is a record of one weighing eleven pounds. This specimen was taken in northwestern Maine. Averages three quarters of a pound to one pound and a half in the streams, and one pound to three pounds in the lakes and ponds. Occurs between latitude 32-1/2° and 55°, in the lakes and streams of the Atlantic watershed, near the sources of a few rivers flowing into the Mississippi and the Gulf of Mexico, and some of the southern affluents of Hudson Bay, its range being limited by the western foothills of the Alleghanies, extending about three hundred miles from the coast, except about the Great Lakes, in the northern tributaries of which it abounds. It also inhabits the headwaters of the Chattahoochee, in the southern spurs of the Georgia Alleghanies and tributaries of the Catawba in North Carolina, and clear waters of the great islands 8 of the Gulf of St. Lawrence—Anticosti, Cape Breton. Prince Edward, and Newfoundland; and abounds in New York, Michigan, Connecticut, Pennsylvania. Maine, Long Island, Canada, Wisconsin, New Hampshire, and Massachusetts. For the larger specimens use a six-ounce fly rod; for the tiny mountain specimens, a four-ounce fly rod. Leaders: Single, fine, and long. Reel: Small click. Flies: 6 to 14 on the streams and 4 to 6 on the lakes and ponds. Patterns: Quaker, Oak, Coachman, Dark Stone, Red Hackle. Blue Bottle, Bradford, Wren, Cahil, Brown Drake. Brandreth, Canada, Page, Professor, Codun, Dark Coachman, and the Palmers—green, gray, red, and brown. Use dark colors on bright days and early in the season; lighter shades on dark days, in the evening, and as the season grows warmer.

Trout, Crescent Lake Blue-Back (Salmo beardsleei): Beardslee Trout, etc. A deep-water fish weighing up to fourteen pounds, found only in Crescent Lake. Washington, and taken during April, May, June, and October, chiefly on the troll. Leaps from the water when hooked. Color: Upper, deep blue ultramarine; lower, white.

Trout, Crescent Lake Long-Headed (Salmo bathæcetor): Closely related to the Steel-Head Trout. A deep-water fish of Lake Crescent, Washington, caught only on set lines within a foot of the bottom. Will not come to the surface; will not take the fly or trolling spoon. Somewhat resembles the speckled trout of Crescent Lake, though more slender and of lighter color.

Trout, Crescent Lake Speckled (Salmo crescentis): Closely resembles the Steel-Head. Weighs up to ten pounds. Found in Crescent Lake, Washington. An excellent game fish.

Trout, Dublin Pond (Salvelinus agassizii): Inhabitant of Center and Dublin Pond and Lake Monadnock, etc., New Hampshire. Differs from the Brook Trout in being pale gray in color and more slender. Reaches a length of eight inches. Brook Trout tackle.

Trout, Green-Back (Salmo stomias): A small black-spotted species, inhabiting the head waters of the Arkansas and Platte rivers; abundant in brooks, streams, and shallow parts of lakes. Common in the waters near Leadville and in Twin Lakes, Colorado, in company with the Yellow-Fin Trout, which see. Weighs up to one pound.

Trout, Greenland (Canada Sea Trout): Caught in midsummer on medium Brook Trout tackle in Labrador, the rivers of considerable size in Canada, and the lakes of Greenland. Rivals the Atlantic Salmon in size, and is a fine sporting species. Averages two pounds in weight. It frequents the sandy pits that are uncovered at half-tide. Higher up the rivers it is found in the pools.

Trout, Jordan's (Salmo jardani): Lake Southerland Spotted Trout, etc. Inhabits Lake Southerland, west of Puget Sound. Caught on the artificial fly as late as October, and is a great leaper. Is black-spotted. Resembles the Utah Trout in color and the Steel-head Trout in shape.

Trout, Kamloops (Salmo kamloops): Stit-tse, etc. A form of the Steel-Head. Abounds in Okanogan, 10 Kamloops, Kootenai lakes, and other waters tributary to the Frazer and upper Columbia rivers. Taken chiefly on the troll. A large, gamy, graceful, slender fish. Color: Dark olive above, bright silvery below.

Trout, Lac de Marbre (Salvelinus marstoni): Marston Trout, etc. Found in Lac de Marbre, near Ottawa, the lakes of the Lake St. John district, Lac à Cassette in Rimouski county, and Lake Soccacomi and the Red Lakes in Maskinonge County, Canada. Takes the fly readily. Color: Upper, dark brown; below, whitish pink unspotted. Reaches a length of one foot.

Trout, Lake (Togue, Fresh-Water Cod, Tuladi. Lunge, etc.): Caught on medium tackle with the troll and minnow bait in deep water, and, early in the season, near the surface, the young rising to artificial trout flies in rapid water. Occurs in all the great lakes of New Brunswick and in many similar waters in Maine. Attains a weight of twenty-one pounds. Haunts deep water as a rule, though often steals to the shoals and shores in search of food, small fish, early in the morning and at twilight.

Trout, Lak (Siscowet, Siskawitz): Caught on medium tackle and small-fish bait along the north shores of Lake Superior. Haunts deep water and feeds upon a species of sculpin. Attains a weight of thirty pounds; averages four pounds. Its habits closely resemble those of the Mackinaw Lake Trout.

Trout, Lake (Mucqua, Bear Trout, etc.): Caught in deep water on medium tackle and small-fish bait on the south shore of Lake Superior. Closely resembles

Oquassa Brown Yellowstone Saibling

11

the Siscowet Lake Trout of the same lake, if it is not, as many think, merely a local variety of the same form.

Trout, Lake (Winipiseogee Trout): Caught on medium tackle and small-fish bait in Lake Winipiseogee and supposedly in Lake George.

Trout, Lake (Mackinaw Trout, Namaycush, Lake Salmon, Salmon Trout, etc.): Caught with medium tackle on the troll and with minnow bait in deep water in the chain of Great Lakes from Superior to Ontario, also in Lake Champlain, New York, and other lakes of the United States and British America, occurring also to the northeastward, in Mackinaw River and in the Knowall River, Alaska. Is known as Mackinaw Trout in Lakes Huron, Michigan, and Superior, and as Lake Salmon and Salmon Trout in the lakes of northern New York. Is said to attain a weight of ninety pounds and a length of six feet.

Trout, Malma (Dolly Varden Trout, Bull Trout. Speckled Trout, Lake Trout, Red-Spotted Trout. Salmon Trout, Chewagh, etc.): Caught on Brook Trout tackle in fresh water and Black Bass tackle in the ocean. Occurs in northern California, west of the Cascade Range, throughout the Aleutian Islands, and northward to Colville River in Alaska, and is not unknown at Behring Island, and Plover Bay, Siberia. Taken in the sea it is called Salmon Trout; in the lakes it is called by all the names parenthesized above. In salt water it feeds upon shrimp, smelt, young trout, sand lance, anchovy, herring, etc.; in fresh water 12 small fish, worms, etc. Weighs up to fourteen pounds in the ocean; averages smaller in the lakes.

Trout, Oquassa (Blue-Back Trout): Caught on Brook Trout tackle in the lakes of western Maine. New York, and New Hampshire. Attains a length of ten inches.

Trout, Saibling: Caught on Brook Trout tackle in Massachusetts, New York, New Hampshire, and Wisconsin. A native of northwestern Europe, introduced in American Brook Trout waters.

Trout, Sunapee (Salvelinus aureolus): American Saibling, White Trout, Golden Trout, Charr, etc. A native of Sunapee Lake, N. H., and Flood Pond. Ellsworth, Maine, now being introduced in other lakes. Favors deep water; takes live bait. Weighs up to twelve pounds.

Trout, Utah (Salmo virginalis): Abounds in the streams and lakes of Utah west of the Wasatch Mountains—in Utah Lake and the Sevier, Jordan, Bear, and Provo rivers. Weighs up to twelve pounds.

Trout, Yellow-Fin (Salmo macdonaldi): Found in Twin Lakes, Colorado, in company with the Green-Back Trout, from which it is distinct in color, habits, and size. Weighs up to nine pounds. Is caught on the artificial fly and with the troll. Favors gravel bottom in deep water.

Trout, Yellowstone (Salmo lewisi): Abundant in Yellowstone Lake, Wyoming, and throughout the

Rainbow Tahoe Steel-head

13

Snake River Basin above Shoshone Falls, and the headwaters of the Missouri.

Salmon Trout, Black-Spotted (Silver Trout, Black Trout, Black-Spotted Trout, Preestl, etc.): Caught on the artificial fly in the Rocky Mountain region, the lakes of New Mexico, Utah, Western Colorado, Wyoming. Idaho, Montana, Oregon, and Washington. The young are abundant in Puget Sound, and are occasionally taken along the California coast. Weighs up to thirty pounds.

Salmon Trout, Brown (Brown Trout, etc.): Caught on the artificial fly practically the same as Brook Trout are taken. Same rods, tackle, and flies. Introduced in this country from Europe. Weighs up to twenty pounds.

Salmon Trout, Kansas River: Caught on Brook Trout tackle from the Kansas River to the upper Missouri. Reaches twenty-four inches in length.

Salmon Trout, Lake Southerland (Salmo declivifrons): Found only in Lake Southerland. Reaches a length of ten inches; is very gamy; takes the fly, and leaps.

Salmon Trout, Lake Tahoe (Lake Tahoe Trout, Silver Trout, Black Trout, etc.): Caught in Lake Tahoe. Pyramid Lake, and the streams of the Sierra Nevada on Brook Trout tackle. Weighs up to twenty pounds.

Salmon Trout, Loch Leven (Loch Leven Trout, etc.): Introduced to this country from Europe, in streams in 14 Michigan, Maine, and other States. Is taken on the artificial fly the same as Brook Trout.

Salmon Trout, Rainbow (Rainbow Trout, Golden Trout, Golden Salmon, Brook Trout, Speckled Trout. Mountain Trout, etc.): Caught with the artificial fly in fresh streams and salt rivers. Occurs from near the Mexican line to Oregon and has been successfully introduced in the Eastern and Northern States, where it is taken upon ordinary Brook Trout tackle—light fly rod, fine leader, click reel, etc. Flies, same as those flailed for Brook Trout. Season: Same as Brook Trout. Weighs up to six pounds.

Salmon Trout, Rio Grande: Abundant in the headwaters of the Rio Grande, Rio Colorado, and their tributaries; occurs in Bear River and the streams of Utah.

Salmon Trout, Steel-Head (Hard-Head, Steel-Head Trout, etc.): Caught mostly in nets. Reaches a weight of twenty-two pounds. Found along the Pacific coast from the Sacramento River northward to Alaska. Abundant in the Columbia and Frazer rivers in the spring. Inhabits river-mouths.

Salmon Trout, Waha Lake (Waha Lake Trout, etc.): Caught on Brook Trout tackle. A local form of the Black-Spotted Salmon Trout, found in Waha Lake, a landlocked mountain tarn in Washington.

15

CHAPTER III

THE ANGLER AND THE FISHERMAN

One profound proof of the soundness in the philosophy that teaches against wantonly wasteful slaughter in the chase is the disinclination on the part of certain so-called sportsmen—a vulgar gentry that resort to the woods and waters solely because it is fashionable to do so—and their guides to honorably dispose of their game after the killing. These greedy snobs are viciously adverse to losing a single bird or fish in the pursuit, but they think little of letting the game rot in the sun after the play. With this fact easily provable any day in the year, it may be said that outside of market fishing and camp fishing for the pot the one real object in fishing and angling is the pursuit itself and not the quarry.

In baseball, it's the game, not the bases; in archery, it's the straightest shooting, not the target. True, we play cards for prizes, but surely as much for the game itself, not altogether for the prizes, because it is possible to buy the prizes or their equivalent outright or take the prizes by force.

My bayman develops fits bordering closely upon incurable hysteria if I lose a single bluefish in the play, but he worries not when he goes ashore with a sloopful of hand-liners and half a hundred fish he cannot make good use of.

16

"Pull it in! you'll lose it!" "We could catch a hundred if you wouldn't fool!" "The other boats'll beat us badly!" "There's a million right 'round the boat!"

These are a few of his excitable expressions. But, when I say to him, "What's the difference, Captain, in losing one or two fish here and wasting half a hundred on shore?" he calms down for a minute or two. Only for a minute or two, however, for he's in the game solely for fish, not the fishing. It's all numbers and size with him, and he's encouraged in this greed by nine out of every ten men he takes aboard his boat.

"We caught fifty," says Tom.

"We caught a hundred and ten," says Dick.

"We caught two hundred and sixty," says Harry.

And so the bayman brags, too, because it's purely business with him.

I have always found the greatest pleasure in fishing is the fishing and not the blood and bones associated with the pursuit. I would rather take five fair fish on fine tackle correctly manipulated than fill the hold with a hundred horrid monsters mastered by mere strength, as in hand-line trolling for bluefish in the ocean and for muskellonge, etc., in fresh water.

"But," says Captain Getemanyway, "I can catch more fish with a hand-line than you can with your fine rod and reel."

"Of course you can," I reply, "and you could catch more if you used a net, a stick of dynamite, or a shotgun."

If it's the fish alone that is the object of the Angler's eye, why resort to any sort of tackle when there's a fish stall in every bailiwick?

17

There is great need of enlightenment in the common ethics of angling. Many persons are under the impression that quantity rather than quality makes the Angler's day.

According to their view of the pursuit, fishing is judged by figures, as in finance— glory to the man with the biggest balance. This is not so, because with this view accepted, Rockefeller would shine above Christ, Shakespeare, and Lincoln.

The mere catch—the number of fish taken—is only one little detail; it is not all of angling. If it were, the superior fisherman would be the man who got his fish in any manner.

Some of our greatest Anglers purposely never excel in the matter of numbers. The Angler's true qualities are based on the application of correct tackle, correct methods in fishing, and a correct appreciation of the pursuit, the game, the day, and the craft.

'Tis the day and the play, not the heads and hides that count.

An ancient writer says of the royal hounds: "The hunter loves to see the hounds pursue the hare, and he is glad if the hare escapes." So it is in angling; we do not wish to catch all the fish we can take in any fashion. We want to take some of them in a proper manner with appropriate implements.

"I can catch more trout with the angleworm and more bass with the trolling spoon than you can with the artificial fly," says Robert.

"Of course you can, Robert," say I, "and you could catch still more if you spread a screen across the tiny stream or set a trap, or if you used a set line with a hundred hooks, just as the target shooter might more readily puncture the circle with a charge of shot than 18 with the single bullet, or just as the greedyman with a blunderbuss might excel in number the wing shot by potting quail bunched on the ground instead of chivalrously bagging single birds on the wing with a pertinent arm."

The neophyte always confounds the angler with the indiscriminate fisherman and so implicates the angler in the cruelty and wastefulness associated with mere chance fishing, when in fact the Angler is the real propagator and protector of the fishes, and is in no sense cruel or wasteful.

The laws that prohibit greedy catches, and protect the mother fish in breeding time, are made by, enforced by, and supported financially by the Angler.

The rearing of the fishes that are placed in depleted waters was originated by, is conducted by, and is paid for by the Angler.

No other class has earnestly bothered its head, honestly lifted its hands, or liberally opened its purse in these matters, and the nearest association man in general has with the preservation of both wild fish and fowl is in uttering a cowardly, false accusation against the one who really deserves sole credit for the work, the sportsman, the genuine field sportsman, not the vicious sporting man of the race track, cockpit, and gambling den— two distinct species of animal, as vastly separated in character as the deerhound and the dragon.

And why this charge against the innocent? Simply because the guilty wish to shield and profit themselves, as the thief cries fire that he may pick your pocket in the panic that ensues.

But then there is a well meaning but wholly unenlightened element, that, influenced by the cry of the 19 methodical spoiler, ignorantly condemns the honest man—the really humane men and women who are sincere in their condemnation but totally ignorant of their subject.

One of this sort, an estimable woman in public life, loudly preaches against the chase and is all the time drawing dividends that provide her with the means to indulge in the vulgarest and cruelest of fashionable extravagances—among them the wool of the unborn lamb, furs from the backs of fast-disappearing quadrupeds, and feathers of the farmers' most valuable insect-destroying song birds—and these wicked dividends derived from several acid factories, a gas house, a power plant, and a dye works that have not only killed off the trillions of fishes in several rivers but destroyed forever the very habitat of the species!

Another of this sort is well exemplified in the character of an old gentleman in Pennsylvania who loudly proclaims against trout fishing, but who utterly ruins nearly eight miles of trout water, once the home of thousands of lordly fish, by permitting his mill hands to run off sawdust in the streams.

This poor, ignorant soul objects to you and me chivalrously taking half a dozen specimens on the fly—catching the cunning trout with an imitation of the living thing itself destroys by the thousands for food and play—while he mercilessly slaughters the entire immediate supply, and prevents further propagation of the whole species with the refuse of his forest-devastating, money-making machine.

True, the Angler like all fishermen, and like the fishes themselves, kills his specimens, but this killing is ordained by nature herself—at least it has better grounds for excuse, if excuse it needs, than that ten-fold 20 more destructive killing by the fishes that not only slay for food, but actually mutilate millions upon millions of their kind for the mere play afforded them in this practice—and though the Angler may be in the wrong when he humanely dispatches a few of the batch he breeds, he is not as hopeless as the wanton fisher, or as brutal as the unenlightened "reformers," the so-called humane lady with the fashionable furs and feathers of fast-disappearing species she never turns a hair to replenish or protect, and the old gentleman hypocrite with his murderous sawmill.

21

CHAPTER IV

FLY-FISHING

"Of all sports, commend me to angling; it is the wisest, virtuousest, best."—Thomas Hood.

When I go fishing, it is for the purpose of catching fish; when I go angling—fly-fishing—it is the soul I seek to replenish, not the creel.

"One of the charms of angling," says Pritt, "is that it presents an endless field for argument, speculation, and experiment."

True, but Anglers have no argument in the first feature of their pastime—the object of it. Fishermen and men who do not go fishing or angling argue that the object sought by the Angler is the fish, but Anglers all agree that the game is but one of the trillion of pleasant things that attract them to the pursuit of it.

They argue and speculate and experiment in the matter of rods and tackle, and they argue as to the virtues of the various species, the qualities of the waters, the conditions of the weather, but they have ever been and ever will be calmly agreed as to the object of it all—the love of studying rather than destroying the game, the love of the pursuit itself.

They angle because of its healthfulness, and the consequent exhilaration of mind and body that attends the gentle practice, not merely for the fishes 22 it may procure them, or for the sake of killing something, as the unenlightened person charges, for the death of an animal, to the Angler, is the saddest incident of his day.

All things animate, man included, were made to kill and to be killed. The only crimes in killing are in killing our own kind, and in killing any kind inhumanly.

And, of all creatures, the Angler is the least offender in these crimes. The very game he seeks, though beautiful and gentle to the eye, and, at times, noble in deed and purpose, is the most brutal killer of all the races—the lovely trout in its attacks upon gaudy flies, the valiant bass and pike in devouring their smaller brethren, and the multitudinous sea-fishes, not alone in their feeding upon one another, but in their wanton murder of the millions upon millions of victims of their pure love of slaughter.

But, of fly-fishing for brook trout:

"Fly-fishing," says Dr. Henshall, "is the poetry of angling"; and "the genuine Angler," says Frederick Pond, "is invariably a poet."

Fly-fishing, the highest order of angling, is indulged in in several forms—in fresh water for salmon, trout, black bass, grayling, perch, pike-perch, pickerel (Long Island brook pickerel), sunfish, roach, dace, shad, herring (branch), etc.; in brackish water for shad, trout, white perch, etc.; and in salt water for bluefish (young), herring (common), mackerel, and—doubt not, kind sir, for I am prepared to prove it—squeteague (weakfish), plaice (fluke, summer flounder), and other species of both bottom and surface habitats—another "endless field for argument, speculation, and experiment."

23

As there are many forms of fly-fishing, so are there many ways of fly-fishing for trout, and many kinds of trout, the various forms of brook trout, lake trout, and sea trout.

Volumes would be required to discourse intelligently upon all these forms of trout and fly-fishing for them; so I purpose in this particular instance to confine myself to one species and one form of trout and one order of fly-fishing.

The trout referred to is the true brook trout, scientifically alluded to as Salvelinus fontinalis and commonly called, besides brook trout (its most popular name), speckled trout, mountain trout, speckled beauty, spotted trout, etc.

The fly-fishing treated of is that popular form that is most indulged in by the Eastern trout fly-fisherman—small-stream fishing in the mountains and wooded level lands that "carries us," as Davy wrote as far away as 1828, "into the most wild and beautiful scenery of nature to the clear and lovely streams that gush from the high ranges of elevated hills."

Above all other styles of fly-fishing, it calls for the most delicate tackle and the very daintiest hand.

"How delightful," says the author of Salmonia, "in the early spring, after the dull and tedious time of winter, when the frosts disappear and the sunshine warms the earth and waters, to wander forth by some clear stream, to see the leaf bursting from the purple bud, to scent the odors of the bank perfumed by the violet, and enameled, as it were, with the primrose and the daisy; to wander upon the fresh turf below the shade of trees, whose bright blossoms are filled with the music of the bee; and on the surface of the waters to view the gaudy flies sparkling like animated 24 gems in the sunbeams, whilst the bright and beautiful trout is watching them from below; to hear the twittering of the water-birds, who, alarmed at your approach, rapidly hide themselves beneath the flowers and leaves of the water-lily; and, as the season advances, to find all these objects changed for others of the same kind, but better and brighter, till the swallow and the trout contend as it were for the May fly, and till in pursuing your amusement in the calm and balmy evening you are serenaded by the songs of the cheerful thrush, performing the offices of paternal love in thickets ornamented with the rose and woodbine."

The other forms of fly-fishing for trout, the pursuit of larger specimens of the same species in larger waters, the lakes and ponds and rivers—all equally inviting by their gentle requirements and the "beautiful scenery of nature"—deserve special treatment, because, as in fly-fishing for salmon (salmo salar), the very top notch of all forms of angling, the play, the player, the scenes, and the accessories are sufficiently different to confound the reader I am mainly endeavoring to amuse with these particular lines.

Small stream fly-fishing for brook trout belongs in a class just between fly-fishing for the brook trout of broader waters, the lakes and ponds, and fly-fishing for salmon in the lordly rivers of Maine and Canada.

The brook trout is angled for in the spring and summer, principally with the artificial fly, and by the chivalric Angler only with the artificial fly, though many greedy fishermen of trifling experience and wholly deprived of the true spirit of angling—in that they fish for the fish alone and judge their day and play solely by the size of their catch—contrive to convince us that the live lure is equally honorable, 25 notwithstanding that the cruel, clumsy, uncleanly, unfair, wasteful practice of live-bait trout fishing is condemned by every truly gentle disciple and practical authority.

Most advocates of live-bait trout fishing, who would have us believe that their method is entitled to recognition in the same category with fly-fishing, proudly proclaim that this should be because they "can catch more fish with the worm or minnow than the Angler can catch with his fly."

If this reasoning is to settle the debate, if killing and quantity compose the Angler's axiom, why not resort to still more productive means—dynamite, or net the stream instead of gently fishing it?

No, the trout fly-fisherman abhors trout bait-fishing for the same reason the wing shot prefers his appropriate arm to a cannon; the yachtsman, his gentle craft to a man-o'-

war; the horseman, his trained mount to a locomotive; the archer, his arrow instead of a harpoon; and so I might go on in similes that would burlesque every form of recreative amusement in the world.

The brook trout breeds in the autumn, favors eddies, riffles, pools, and deep spots under the banks of the stream, and near rocks and fallen trees, and feeds on flies, small fish, worms, and other small life forms.

Its shape, weight, size, and color are influenced by its food, its age, its activity, its habitat, and its habits. Its color corresponds to the color of the water bottom and will change as the water bottom changes. If removed to a new water, where the bottom color is different from the bottom color of its first abode—lighter or darker, as the case may be,—it will gradually grow to a corresponding shade, blending with its new 26 habitat just as its colors suited the stones and grasses and earthy materials of its native domain.

In weight, the brook trout ranges up to ten pounds in large waters. There is a record of one weighing eleven pounds. This specimen was taken in Northwestern Maine. The species averages threequarters of a pound to one pound and a half in the streams, and one pound to three pounds in the lakes and ponds. It occurs between latitude 32-1/2° and 55°, in the lakes and streams of the Atlantic watershed, near the sources of a few rivers flowing into the Mississippi and the Gulf of Mexico, and some of the southern affluents of Hudson Bay, its range being limited by the western foothills of the Alleghanies, extending about three hundred miles from the coast, except about the Great Lakes, in the northern tributaries of which it abounds. It also inhabits the headwaters of the Chattahoochee, in the southern spurs of the Georgia Alleghanies, and tributaries of the Catawba in North Carolina and clear waters of the great islands of the Gulf of St. Lawrence—Anticosti, Cape Breton, Prince Edward, and Newfoundland; and abounds in New York, Michigan, Connecticut, Pennsylvania, Maine. Long Island, Canada, Wisconsin, New Hampshire, and Massachusetts.

My favorite rod for stream trout fishing is a cork-handled, all-lancewood rod of three or four ounces in weight and eight feet in length, or a rod of similar length weighing four or five ounces and made of split bamboo—the best split bamboo of the best workmanship. The cheap, so-called split bamboo of the dry-goods store bargain (?) counter, retailed for a price that would not pay for the mere wrapping of the correct article, is a flimsy, decorative thing, and would 27 collapse, or, worse still, bend one way and stay that way, if used on the stream. The fly-rod material must be springy and resiliently so, and the rod must be constructed so as to permit of this condition.

The reel I favor is a small, narrow, light, all-rubber or narrow aluminum common-click reel, holding twenty-five yards of the thinnest-calibered silk, waterproof-enameled line.

My leader is a brown-stained one of silk gut, twelve feet in length. The leader should be fresh and firm, flexible and fine, not a dried-up, brittle, unyielding, snappy snarl of the salesman's discarded sample box that breaks at the mere touch, or releases the flies at the first cast or parts at the first strike—if by some miraculous mischance you get this far with it. The leaders, a half-dozen of them, should be carried, when not in actual use, in a flat, aluminum, pocket-fitting box between two dampened flannel mats (though not preserved this way in close season), so as to have them thoroughly limp from being water soaked, that you may more readily and more safely adjust them, for break they surely will if handled in a dry state.

The willow creel, in which the spoil of the day is deposited, should be, I think, about the size of a small hand-satchel. To this is fastened a leather strap, with a broad, shoulder-protecting band of stout canvas. This I sling over the right shoulder, allowing the creel to hang above the back part of the left hip where it will least interfere with me during the fight with fontinalis.

The landing net I use is a little one of egg shape, made of cane with no metal whatsoever, and it has a linen mesh about ten inches in width and eighteen inches in length. The handle is a trifle over one foot 28 in length. To this I tie one end of a stout but light-weight flexible and small-calibered cord, or a stretch of small rubber tube, and the other end of this I tie to a button on my coat under my chin, throwing the net over my left shoulder to lie on my back until called into service.

The clothing should be of dark-gray wool of light weight. I wear a lightly woven gray sweater under my coat when the weather is cool.

I have plenty of pockets in my trouting coat, and I make it a practice to tie a string to nearly everything I carry in them—shears, hook-file, knife, match-box, tobacco-pouch, pipe, purse, field-glasses, fly-book, etc.—so that I will not mislay them ordinarily, or drop them in the rushing current during some exciting moment.

The headgear I like is a gray, soft felt hat of medium brim to protect my eyes in the sun and to sit upon in the shade.

The footwear may consist of waterproof ankle shoes attached to rubber or canvas trousers, or of a pair of light, close-fitting hip rubber boots. Some Anglers wear rubber waterproof combined trousers and stockings and any sort of well-soled shoes. In warm weather, I affect nothing beyond a pair of old shoes with holes cut in both sides to let the water run freely in and out, the holes not big enough to admit sand and pebbles.

The artificial flies are of many hundreds of patterns. I have a thousand or two, but half a hundred, of sizes four to six for the lakes and ponds, and six to fourteen for the small streams, are enough to select from during a season; two dozen are sufficient for a single trip, half a dozen will do to carry to the stream for a day,—if 29 you don't lose many by whipping them off or getting them caught in a tree,—and two are all I use for the cast, though a cast of three flies is the favorite of many fishermen. I amuse myself by presuming to have a special list for each month, week, day, and hour, but the extravagantly erratic notions of the trout forbid my recommending it to brother rodmen. Trout that show a preference for certain flies one day may the next day favor entirely different patterns. Sometimes they will take an imitation of the natural fly upon the water and at other times, being gorged with the natural insect, will only strike at some oddly colored concoction of no resemblance to any living thing in nature; this in play, or in anger, and at other times out of pure curiosity. An Angler doesn't need a great number of flies—if he knows just what fly the game is taking. You can't very well determine this half a hundred miles from the fishing; so you take a variety with you and experiment. The flies should be of the best make and freshest quality, tied by a practical hand—some honest maker who is himself an Angler—not the cheap, dried-up, wall-decorative, bastard butterflies of the ladies' dry-goods shop, that hybrid mess of gaudy waste ribbon-silk and barnyard feather, the swindling output of the catch-penny shopman whose sweat help do not know—upon my word—the name or the purpose of the thing they make.

Any six of the following list will kill well enough for a single day's pleasant fishing in any water at any time during the legal season: Dark Coachman, Gray and Green Palmer, Ginger Palmer, Alder, Scarlet Ibis, Abbey, Imbrie, Professor, Conroy, Reuben Wood, March Brown, Orvis, White Miller, Coachman. Royal Coachman, Codun, Brown and Red Palmer, 30 Brown Hen, Queen of the Water, King of the Water. Squires, Black Gnat, Grizzly King, Quaker.

I use, as a rule, dark colors in clear water, and on bright days and early in the season; lighter shades in dull water and on dark days, in the evening, and as the season grows warmer; but many Anglers philosophize just the reverse—use light colors for early season fishing and somber hues for midsummer play—hence the endless arguments and experiments described as one of the charms of the craft.

I prefer, as I have said, two flies on the leader, and my favorite of favorites for all times and all places is a cast made up of gnat-size pattern of dark-gray wing and pale-blue body, and another of a peculiar drab-cream shade.

In throwing or casting the fly I never "whip" or "flail" the rod, and I never cast with a long line when a short one will answer the purpose. Distance alone may count in a fly-casting contest, but in the wild stream a careful short cast is more effective than a clumsy long one.

I angle with my shadow behind me, and in casting the flies endeavor to allow only the flies to touch the water. The line frightens the game, and if a trout should take a fly on a loose, wavy line, he will not hook himself and he will blow the fly from his mouth before the Angler is able to hook him.

In learning to cast the fly, the young Angler should start with the leader alone, as I believe all fly-fishing is begun by old and young, and as he lifts the flies from the water after the forward cast to make the backward motion he should simultaneously draw from the reel a half-yard of line and allow time for the flies to complete the whole circuit back of him. In 31 fly-fishing the cast is not made from the reel as in bait-casting; the line is drawn from the reel a half-yard at a time with the left hand. The line must fully straighten itself behind the Angler ere it can be sent out straight before him. The flies and at most only a little part of the leader should fall lightly upon the surface—as we imagine two insects, entangled in a delicate cobweb, might fall from a tree branch—and be drawn smartly but gently in little jerks a second or two in imitation of two tiny live-winged bugs fluttering in the water; and then, as the Angler steps slowly, firmly, but silently and softly in the current downstream, he should repeat the lifting of the flies, the drawing off of more line from the reel, and the circling backward cast that takes up the slack and gives the line its forward force. Thus he should continue, deftly placing the lure in every likely spot ahead of him in the center of the brook and along its moss-lined, flower-decked, rock-bound or grass-fringed banks.

The Angler is careful not to let the trout see him, see his shadow, or see the rod, and not to let this wisest, most watchful species of all the finny tribes hear him or feel the vibration of his body.

In hooking the trout the Angler strikes the second the fish strikes—not by a violent arm movement, but by a mere instantaneous nervous backward twist of the wrist, as one would instinctively draw up his hand from the pierce of a needle point. Many trout are hooked the instant the leader is lifted for a new cast, and many hook themselves without the slightest effort on the part of the Angler.

When the fish is hooked he should not be flaunted in the air, as the boy fisher yanks his pond perch. 32 The prize should be handled as if he were but slightly secured, his head should be kept under water, the line kept gently taut, and the fish softly led out of noisy water and away from stones, long grass, submerged tree branches or logs.

If the catch is heavy enough to draw the line from the reel it is allowed to do so, but the line should be kept taut and reeled in the second he hesitates. There need be no hurry.

After a little while the game's rushes will cease; then it should be reeled in, care being taken not to arouse it again by the contact of a weed or stone.

The tip of the rod is now raised over the head and back of the Angler until the butt points downward; then, if the fish has been reeled in near enough, it is secured in the landing net, tail first, and carefully slid into the creel through the little square opening for this purpose in the lid.

If you, reader mine, should some day get as far as this glorious part of the play, and the fish should be a small one, be satisfied; the true Angler is ever of a contented heart; if the fish should be too small, set it free—the true Angler is always humane and generous; if it should prove fit to feed upon, do not subject it to unnecessary suffering—skillfully kill it outright at once; the true Angler is manly and merciful.

And, and—good luck to you, brother.

33

CHAPTER V

WALTON'S WAY

"More than half the intense enjoyment of fly-fishing is derived from the beautiful surroundings."—Charles F. Orvis.

A clause in a recent tariff bill prohibited the importation of some of the favorite artificial flies of the Angler and likewise prohibited the importation of the materials used in making these flies, particularly feathers and skins of the valuable song birds whose insect-eating prevents the destruction of the trees and other foliage absolutely necessary to the preservation of the planet upon which man lives.

This clause was fathered by the wise and welcome bird-protecting institutions known as the Audubon Societies, and was intended to stop the infamous traffic in wild birds for millinery purposes, which, if not reformed, means the utter extermination of the world's feathered friends.

The feathers and skins imported annually for artificial flies were to come under the same prohibition as millinery feathers.

England has a law prohibiting the importation of certain plumage, but specific exception is made for the materials used in fly-making.

There was a foolish opposition to this clause on the part of a few professional fly tiers, some of the fly 34 dealers, and a lot of fishermen, and these men and women were loud in their declaration that the Angler is also opposed to the clause, which, if allowed, they think would injure the business of the professional fly maker, fly dealer, et al.

Now the truth is: No Angler was opposed to the clause, and the claim that the protection of valuable tree-saving birds would hurt trade of any sort is absurd. The same sort of foolish objection was made to the introduction of the sewing-machine—it was said it would prevent a lot of hand-sewing workmen from making a living. In a few years man will laugh at this silly and selfish individual cry against bird-protection with the same ridiculous spirit with which he now laughs at the old idiotic objection to the sewing-machine.

A writer in the New York Sun says: "The first effect of prohibiting the importation of the feathers for flies will be to drive many back to bait-fishing. An Angler using bait should take ten trout for every one he could kill with a fly. The Government, the States, and clubs are spending large sums for the stocking of streams with trout. The expenditure would scarcely be justified if there is to be bait-fishing in these streams—they would soon be fished out. Thousands who formerly used bait have taken up fly-fishing because it is better sport."

What does this writer mean by the word "many"—the "many" he thinks that will be driven back to bait fishing as the effect of the prohibition of the importation of the feathers for flies? Many what? Not Anglers, by any means, because the Angler would rather merely try to catch his trout with an artificial fly made from a feather duster than to be assured of 35 catching the game with a worm or minnow or salmon egg. The "many" refers to fishermen, or professional fly tiers, not Anglers.

The Angler and the ordinary fisherman are as far separated in character and nature as the hummingbird and the buzzard are separated in life and lesson.

The real opposer to bird-protection in this objection to the clause prohibiting the importation of bird feathers and skins is the commercial fellow, and there is no commercial side to angling.

The Angler is a student as well as a lover of nature, and he knows that without the insect-eating birds there can be no trees, that without trees there can be no waters, that without waters there can be no fishes, and that without fishes there can be no fishing. The stupid fisherman can't surmount this, and the commercial fly tier, whose business alone teaches him enough of the angling art to be able to figure this natural science, thinks too much of his money creel to admit it. This pretended ignorance is called good business instinct, and the Angler doesn't object to men minding their own business, but when business instinct runs wild and evokes the effrontery to imply that the Angler, a non-commercial being, is opposed to the prohibition of earth-valuable bird extermination, business instinct is going a little too far with its money-mad method.

The Angler does not condemn the use of correct tackle; he's a believer in it, and just as he is sincere in his advocacy of proper tackle and in his immaculate use of proper tackle, so is he sincere in his profound belief in correct methods in fishing.

The fisherman—the fellow who judges his day by the number of fishes he kills in any manner regardless 36 of season and size—may resort to dynamite, and he may not be in sympathy with any of the chivalric means, manners, and methods of any of the worldly matters, but the Angler is not of this stamp.

Izaak Walton, the father of fishing, never posed for his portrait with half a hundred dead fishes tied to his body. Ferns, feathered friends, flowers, fair skies, fine fishing tackle, and fishes embellished his pictures.

The fish, to the Angler, is only one feature—no doubt the main feature—of his favorite pastime, and the killing of the fish is not a pleasant part of his pursuit; the death of the game is, to the Angler, a sad incident, however happy the fisherman may be over the slaughter of his greedy mess, and the Angler, therefore, could not possibly derive the delights of his angling at the sacrifice of the lordly winged creatures he so repeatedly thanks his Master for.

Who ever read an Angler's story without the song birds in it? The expression "gentle art" is applied to angling and the Angler. Who ever heard of the gentle art of fishing! And angling is a gentle art; so, to practice it, one must be gentle.

The Angler will not resort to fishing with live bait if the few European artificial flies are excluded from his lures, because he can catch all the fishes his gentle art entitles him to with the flies of home make.

The artificial flies of England, Scotland, and Ireland are lovely creations of practical as well as beautiful design, and the Angler adores them, but, since his gentle creel can be filled without them, he'll not insist on their importation if it tends in the slightest manner toward the extermination of the very things that make possible the gentle art of angling— the birds and the trees, without which the fishes themselves could not survive.

37

The world is not composed entirely of fishermen—the earth itself should not be sacrificed for a few against the multitude—and the Angler, the fisherman of quality, is wise enough to appreciate this; his individual pastime is not as important as the general welfare of the masses, and it will be said that the fisherman, who estimates quantity over quality, is far less entitled to consideration.

Angling is a pastime of a craft; the birds, the trees, and the waters are necessities of a planet and its people.

Fishing for the market—a distinct method from that of the Angler and the common fisherman who fishes for the mere sake of killing and counting—is not concerned in this argument, and may be dismissed with a brief word of commendation. Legitimately practiced, discriminately carried on according to the law of man and nature, it is even more admirable than angling and far more honorable than the wasteful pursuit of the vulgar amateur fisherman. Our Saviour sanctioned net fishing; chose simple fishermen for his disciples—St. Andrew, St. Peter, St. James, and St. John.

The expression, "fly fisherman," may refer to the fisherman or the Angler, for there are lots of fly fishermen as well as mere fishermen who are not Anglers, for the reason that fly-fishing, indulged in by a greedy hand, can permit of ungentle fish-catching the same as bait-fishing. Both methods are equally destructive if not followed with strict rules of angling, and all that need be said to properly define angling is that it is the poetry—the art and refinement—of fishing. The common fisherman is simply a fish-basket filler; the Angler fills his soul, not the creel.

38

CHAPTER VI

THE WANTON WAY

"There's an Angler's law, and a court or legal law. The fisherman who adheres to the Angler's law can't break the court law."—Seth Fielding.

Gentility in the limit of the catch and giving the fish its sporting chance on light tackle constitute the ethical soul of angling. The fisherman who stops fishing when he has a few specimens is angling; he's an Angler. The fisherman who fishes with no limit in his catch is merely fishing; he's a fisherman, not an Angler.

Any picture of a few fishes may illustrate the catch of the Angler, and the photograph on Frontispiece shows the catch of the worst type of fisherman—the wanton fish exterminator who, ignoring the Angler's gentle law, takes his greedy mess because it is according to the so-called legal law.

Dr. William T. Hornaday, author of Wild Life Conservation, The American Natural History, Our Vanishing Wild Life, etc., and director of the New York Zoölogical Park, has sent me the photograph of the greedyman's catch—made near Spokane, Washington—with the following notes:

"The great trouble [in the matter of wasteful fish-catching is not so much with the people who catch 39 fish as with the brutally destructive laws that permit fishermen to catch four or five times as many fish as they should. There are a great many sportsmen who sincerely believe that it is all right to take all the fish and game of all kinds that the law allows. Whenever any destruction is waged on that basis I always charge it to the abominably liberal laws that in many cases seemed framed to promote destruction. Ninety-nine per cent. of the streams of this country very soon will be so nearly destitute of fish that fishing will become a lost art. In the Rocky Mountains the overfishing abuse is particularly vicious and destructive because in those cold streams the fish mature slowly, their food is very scarce and dear, and the fish are so hungry that they are easily caught. It is an easy matter to completely fish out a mountain stream in the Rocky Mountain region or in the Pacific States. In the State of Wyoming some very aggravated cases of wanton fish destruction by indifferent rod and line fishermen have lately been brought to my attention."

Dr. Hornaday is an Angler, and his views and practices are endorsed by all Anglers. His great book on wild life conservation is brimful of practical detail and should be in the library of all who are interested in the preservation of our fishes, birds, and quadruped game. Here is a sample of the Doctor's vigorous style in his admirable campaign against the exterminator:

"A few years ago, certain interests in Pennsylvania raised a great public outcry against the alleged awful destruction of fish in the streams of Pennsylvania by herons.... A little later on, however, the game commissioners found that the herons remaining in Pennsylvania were far too few to constitute a pest to fish life, and furthermore, the millinery interests 40 appeared to be behind the movement. Under the new law the milliners were enabled to reopen in Pennsylvania the sale of aigrettes, because those feathers came from members of the unprotected Heron Family! It required a tremendous State campaign to restore protection to the herons and bar out the aigrettes; but it was accomplished in 1912. Hereafter, let no man for one moment be deceived by the claim that the very few-and-far-between herons, bitterns, and kingfishers that now remain in the United States, anywhere, are such a menace to fish life that those birds are a pest and deserve to be shot. The inland streams of the United States and Canada lack fishes because they have been outrageously overfished,—wastefully, wickedly depleted, without sense or reason, by men who scorn the idea of conservation. In Orleans County, New York, a case was reported to me of a farmer who dynamited the waters of his own creek, in spawning time!"

The Angler angles according to his own humanely conservative law. The greedy fisherman fishes according to court or so-called legal law, good or bad, and he always breaks the Angler's law and very often the court's law.

In viewing Dr. Hornaday's Spokane photograph note the bait-casting reel on the fly-casting rod—the rig of a clumsy as well as greedy fisherman. The mess of trout shown is one that no Angler would ever make and one that any gentleman would be ashamed of— "three times too many fish for one rod," as Dr. Hornaday says, "another line of extermination according to law." Of course, the Doctor means the fisherman's law or the court's law, not the Angler's law.

CHAPTER VII

FLY-FISHING FOR TROUT

"The variety of rivers require different ways of angling."—Izaak Walton, The Compleat Angler.

The art of catching fish with artificial lures in imitation of natural insects is the most chivalric of all methods of angling.

Fish, particularly trout, often hook themselves when they seize the fly of a fisherman using a pliant rod that will yield and spring freely. As the game strikes, the Angler strikes, hooking the fish swiftly but delicately by a simple turn of the wrist. The trout is not flaunted up in the air by force, as some coarse perch fishermen lift their catch. The trout fisher does not use his arm at all in hooking a trout beyond aiding the hand in holding the rod for the wrist to do the work. A practiced troutman can secure his fish by moving his hand five inches—a little backward nervous twist of the wrist.

Trout often snap a fly and spit it out so quickly that the tyro does not have a chance to strike and hook the prize. At other times they take hold more slowly, and afford the beginner more opportunity to hook them, and, as I have said, they very often hook themselves.

The beginner will have some trouble in overcoming 42 the excitement or "trout fever" that always accompanies the trout's rise and strike, but experience will gradually make him more calm and active at this important moment. The tyro trout fisher is often more frightened at the rise of the trout than he would be at the flush of a noisy grouse or the springing of a surprised deer.

When you have hooked the fish, always handle him as if he were but lightly secured. Do not attempt to lift him out or yank him up to you. Keep the line gently taut, and softly lead the prize out of rough water or away from stones, grasses, logs, or tree branches. Do not let him come to the surface until he is pretty well exhausted and you are about to put him in the landing-net. If he is a large fish, tow him ashore if the water edge will permit. Where there are overhanging banks this cannot be done. Do not be in a hurry to get him out of the water. Be calm and work carefully.

If the fish is large enough to overcome the reel click and run off the line, let him do so, but check him and guide him according to any obstruction there may be.

When he has rushed here and there for some little time with his mouth open and with a constant check—the line should always be taut—he will become tired, and when he is tired he will not rush. Then softly reel him in, being careful not to let him come in contact with a stone or weed, which is sure to arouse him again. Reel him up quickly, without making a splashing swoop, and he will soon grace your creel.

Several persons have expressed an objection to a list of flies I once named, saying a good Angler might kill just as many trout on quarter the number.

43

Any Angler can take even less than one quarter of the enumerated list and catch fully as many brook trout as one who might use all of the flies mentioned—if he can pick out the ones the trout are rising to without trying them all until he discovers the killing ones. A chef might please his master with one or two of the forty courses billed, if he knew what the man wanted.

Sometimes an Angler can judge the appropriate fly to use by observing nature in seeing trout rise to the live fly; but, there are times when trout are not rising, times when they are tired of the fly upon the water, and times when the real fly is not on the wing. Then the Angler is expected to take matters in his own hands and whip about quietly until he discovers the proper patterns. It is better to try for the right flies with a list of twenty-nine than whip over a list of a thousand or more. I have learned from experience that trout, like human beings, are in love with a variety of foods at different times. Their tastes change with the months, the weeks, the days, the hours, and, under certain conditions which I will presently explain, the minutes.

"... fish will not bite constantly, nor every day. They have peculiar, unexplainable moods that continuing favoring conditions of water, wind, and weather cannot control" (Eugene McCarthy, Familiar Fish).

When I mention twenty-nine different patterns as being seasonable at a stated period, I do not mean to say that the trout will rise to them all and at any time and under all conditions. In the first place, the person using them might be a tyro unfamiliar with the gentle art, the streams might be dried up, there might be an earthquake, the flies might be too large, too coarse, 44 and for that matter a thousand other conditions might interfere. I fish dozens of streams in different localities several times every month during the legal season, and I have been a fond Angler—if not a skillful one—since my tenth birthday. Experience on the streams, a true love for nature, and a careful attention to my notebook enable me to separate the artificial flies into monthly lists. No man can class them into weekly or daily lots.

"When a fly is said to be in season it does not follow that it is abroad on every day of its existence" (Alfred Ronalds).

The Eastern gentleman who said if he could have but one fly he would take a yellow one, is probably a good Angler, for a yellow fly is a fair choice. If I could have but one fly I should take a—ah! I cannot name its color; 'tis the quaker, a cream, buff, grayish, honey-yellow shade.

Beaverkill, Seth Green, Ashey Montreal, Dun. Wickham's Fancy, August Brown are killing patterns in the Pennsylvania streams.

Trout change in their tastes by the month, week, day, hour, and minute. There are flies among the list given for this or that month that they will not rise to to-day or perhaps to-morrow, but surely there are some among the list that will please them, and you have to discover those particular flies, and so, as I have said before, 'tis better to search among twenty-nine than twenty-nine hundred.

In July of a certain season I waded a stream in Pennsylvania and had these flies with me: Quaker. Oak, Codun, Reuben Wood, White Miller, Yellow Sallie, Hare's Ear, Iron Dun, Brown Palmer, Cahill, and a few others. The first day I killed eighteen trout 45 in fishing fifty yards in a small stream running partly through a large open field and partly through bushes, fishing from the left bank. Twelve were taken on a brown palmer, four on a dark-gray midge, and two on a tiny yellow-gold-brown fly. I fished three hours, in which time I received exactly two hundred and fifteen strikes; eighteen, as I have said, proved killing. I fished stealthily up and down the stream, hiding here and there and making the most difficult of casts at all times. I went up and down the little stream a half dozen times, never going into the wood, but merely fishing from where the stream came out of the wood to where it hid itself again beyond the field. Part of the water I fished, as I say, was in underbush, but I did not leave the field.

Now I am going to show you how the tastes of trout varied by minutes, in two instances at least, and I desire you to know every little detail. To well convince you that the casts I made were difficult, I will say that my line became fastened in twigs, leaves, and bushes every other toss. I had to put the flies through little openings no larger than the creel head and take chances of getting the leader caught while on the way, and after it was there and on its return. I sometimes whipped twenty times at a little pool before I reached it. There were logs, branches, mosses, cresses, leaves, and grasses to avoid. The water in parts was swift and still, narrow, shallow, and deep, sometimes being four feet wide and three feet deep, and then ten feet wide and three inches deep; sometimes running smartly over bright grasses or pebbles and light in color, and in other places lying dark and still in pools made by logs and deep holes.

A tyro would have fished the ground in ten minutes 46 and caught nothing; some Anglers would have gone over it once in twenty-five minutes and taken a half-dozen fish. I had the day to myself; I had nowhere else to go; I was out for sport, recreation, and study,—not fish, for I am a lover of nature in general,—and so I took three hours at the play, and fished and observed inch by inch like a mink, the king of trouters.

I say I had two hundred and fifteen strikes, out of which I killed eighteen trout, and you are surprised. You think you could have done better, much better, but I know you could not—you could not have done as well as I did and I wish that I could put you to a test. I have seen a fontinalis rise to a small coachman twenty-six times, snapping apparently at the feather each time, but never allowing himself to be hooked nor hooking himself. He was playing. He was a young trout, but an educated one, and well knew there was no danger if he kept his wits about him. I have witnesses to this performance who will substantiate my story, and I can easily further prove the truthfulness of the statement by taking you to a stream where a similar performance may be enacted. And I have seen an uneducated trout rise and snap at a fly without taking it. The first one rose in play, this one in curiosity—and there are trout that will rise in anger. All of them may know the bait is not food. It is a mistake to think that all brook trout will spurt from a fly the very second they discover it is not real food, as it is an error to believe that all brook trout will take the fly when they know it is the living thing. All trout are not alike; they vary in their tastes and antics as they do in color and size. Mind you, I speak only of one species here—the true brook trout, Salvelinus fontinalis, and thus the material should be interesting.

Taking the fly
AN UNUSUAL WAY OF TAKING THE FLY

47

The day I took my creel of eighteen was a fair one; we had rain the day before; the water was clear and the stream was in ordinary condition. The brown hackle which killed twelve of the eighteen was on a No. 8 hook; the other two flies were tied on No. 16, as the hackle should have been, for the fish were small and the stream was in a small-fly condition and quite right for the daintiest leaders and the finest midges. But the hackle seemed to please the trout; all sizes appeared to jump at it. I hooked many that were not over three inches long! Several times when taking my flies from the water for a new cast, I lifted a poor little trout up in the air back of me, like the scurvy fisherman who makes a practice of landing all his fish by yanking them out. So you see it pays to be patient on the stream and try all sorts of gentle tricks with fontinalis. You must not hurry; you must not be coarse; you must not be careless and untidy with your fly-book. Take your time, fish slowly, surely, and delicately. Be not weary of the play: banish the thought of discouragement, keep at the sport for sport alone, and study as you angle.

A little trout will rise to a fly he has missed one or more times; a large trout will seldom do so. When you miss a big trout do not give him back the fly for ten minutes, and then if you miss him again, change the pattern, wait a little while, and he is once more ready for the rise—if the new fly suits him.

I never raised a trout on the scarlet ibis fly. I believe it is a poor color on the well-fished waters, just as I believe that all flies are killing on wild streams. New trout will take old flies; old trout love new ones and many old ones. Personally I like the sober colors in flies for all seasons on all water, though I well 48 appreciate the old rule: "When the day is bright and where the water is clear, small flies and plain colors; in deep and dull waters and on dark days and in the evening the brighter and larger ones." Trout do not in all cases show their liking to flies in accordance with any condition of weather or water, though as a rule it is advisable to use lighter colors when the day and water are dull, which is not saying, however, that fish will not rise to loud flies on bright days or sober flies in dull weather, for the tastes of trout vary like the tastes of other living things, and nothing can equal them in erraticness when fly-feeding.

You must give fontinalis sport, for he very often strikes for play more than food, and, like every other living thing, loves a choice of variety.

There is an old story that if the Angler's book has a pattern of fly in exact imitation of the real fly upon the trout water, he has but to join it as the stretcher to fill his creel. Ogden tells us in so many words: "Give not the trout an exact imitation of the real fly upon the water, for your artificial fly will then be one in a thousand. Something startling will please them better—loud gold body, strange-colored wings—and an odd fellow may take it for sport if nothing else."

While this is a good bit of advice, it does not seem right to me to send it forth in such a sweeping manner. The question of whether we should imitate nature in general fly building has long been in vogue. Some say we should do so, and others that it does not matter. Both are correct—there are times when we should copy the living flies, and times when we should use those artificial things that have no resemblance to nature's insects. I have come upon a water where the trout were rising to the small dusky miller, and 49 have, by putting on the artificial fly of this order, taken a dozen beauties in good play. It was because I arrived just in time; the trout were not tired of their course. Perhaps twenty minutes later they would not have done more than eyed my cast. In that case, even if the water were covered with a species of the real fly, it would have been better to have offered something different. Copy nature if the fish be devouring—not alone because the fly is on the water; they may be tired of it. Sometimes there are flies being taken that are not seen by the Angler, for trout can snap a fly upon the wing. Fly-fishing is not an easy pursuit; 'tis a real science. Rules are good, but we must not fail to suit the rules to conditions.

No; you are not supposed to use the entire list, for to-day the trout may not favor over two or three of them; to-morrow he may take six of them—all different from those he may show a liking for to-day. It is all very well for an Angler to take but three dozen coachmen and brown and gray hackle for the Western trout, or any trout that is not educated up to the standard of the trout that is fished for incessantly, but I should not like to make a month's trouting trip and take along only three kinds of flies, even if I had dozens of each of the three and if my favorite quaker were one of the trio, no matter where the stream—East. West, North, or South.

Some days after my catch of eighteen I visited the field again and fished from the point where the stream entered the wood down to a beautiful little waterfall. I took twenty-one of fair size—one on a yellow Sallie, one on an oak fly, four on an Esquimaux dun, five on a hare's ear, and nine on the quaker. This day I had ninety-three rises—not as many as on the day I took 50 the eighteen and had two hundred and fifteen rises. The day was dark, the water very clear and shallow, and there had been no rain for ten days.

This was the occasion of learning more about striking the Eastern brook trout than I had ever before enjoyed. The old rule is to strike on the second of the rise, and, while I do not think this electric quickness should be practiced in all cases and under all conditions. I found it was the rule this day, especially in the one deep pool I found. In other places—one in particular, where I saw six of my catch make every move in taking the flies—I found it necessary to depart from the old rule and strike not upon the second of the rise. I very often gave wrist too quickly. It all goes to prove that rules are not to be exercised at all times and under all conditions. We must make allowances. I came upon one quiet piece of water that was as clear and still as glass; I could see every detail of the pebbles at the bottom. Eight pretty trout were in this bed of silent water, resting without a perceptible movement—not even that delicate wave of the tail so common with the trout in his balancing in running water. They did not see me; a bush hid my form. When my slender rod tip moved over the water and the leader with the flies went down gently upon the surface, the trout thought (all animals think) the wind had stirred the frail branch of an adjacent tree and swept into the water upon a cobweb three insects for their feeding. Four rushed for the deceit and two were hooked quietly and quickly. I landed them and went away to return to the same spot a half-hour later. Seven trout were there this time. I flailed gently over them, but received no rushing rise; one little fellow came up deliberately, broke water two inches 51 behind the little dun, and then returned to his old position. Then two others did precisely the same as their companion had done, excepting one that chose the oak fly for his inspection. Then they sank themselves, and a fourth gamester spurted up to the dun and took it in his mouth much as a sunfish would suck in a bit of worm. I struck him, and he made a splash that nearly drove a near-by-perched catbird into hysterics, and sent the other trout up, down, and across the stream like so many black streaks of lightning. Now, had I cast at these fish from above or below and not just over them, where I saw every move they made, I should have given them wrist on the second of their rise—as I did in the case of the first two that made the first rush—and lost any chance of success.

No, I say, we must not always follow rules regardless of conditions. We must not judge all trout alike, even if they be of one species. Men, though of one race, are not all alike in their habits any more than they are in their sizes and colors.

I found in some parts of the stream that as long as I changed the flies I had rises; in other parts no trout took the fly, no matter how I worked it. Perhaps there were no fish hereabout; perhaps they saw me; perhaps they were not hungry, and perhaps there were hundreds and thousands of other reasons why they were not to be taken in these certain places.

No man can strictly follow rules in all cases and take trout upon every occasion of his trials. Conditions govern, and must be studied—conditions, conditions.

52

CHAPTER VIII

THE ANGLER'S PRAYER—SAVE THE WOODS AND WATERS

"Perpetual devotion to what a man calls his business is only to be sustained by perpetual neglect of other things. And it is not by any means certain that a man's business is the most important thing he has to do."
Robert Louis Stevenson.

Commerce or civilization or whatever you like to call modern man's accumulation of money wealth at the sacrifice of nature is perpetrated with no greater force than in the wanton waste of our forests—the trees given by God to the people and stolen from the people by individuals. It seems all right for man to prudently use our forests in the making of homes and other practical things of actual necessity, but it is a downright shame that the people allow greedy men to destroy the trees for the mere sake of adding dollars to the destroyers' already well-filled purses. And these selfish men even deprive the people of their breathing-air, drinking-water, and fish food. Springs, ponds, and brooks are dried up by the loss of sheltering foliage. Lakes and rivers are ruined by the commercial gentry's waste acid, dye, oil, gas, etc., and the very air we breathe is poisoned by the fumes of the money-makers' chimneys.

The railroads cut down the people's trees to make ties, and they burn the old ties instead of consuming 53 them for steam power or giving them back to the people for fuel or fence posts, etc. The mill owner burns as rubbish the sawdust and slabs instead of burying the sawdust and allowing it to turn into loam that would enrich the soil and thereby propagate vegetable food matter and the very tree life the millman wastes. He is not only destroying the material on hand but he is doing his best to prevent the growth of future material. Slabs should not be burned as waste matter; they are good fuel and good material for the farmer, et al.

Nothing should be burned as waste matter; nature tells us to bury, not burn. Fire destroys not alone the valuable ingredient it consumes to make itself, but burns up the earth's vital moisture—the life-giving oxygen we breathe, without which no animate thing could survive.

Before fresh timber is cut for market-cornering purposes, the millmen should be compelled to use up the vast rafts of trees they have allowed to float upon river banks, there to rot while the choppers continue their attack on new trees, half of which will go to waste with the lumberman's already-decaying market-cornering mess in the flooded valley.

Anyone may personally witness this wanton waste if so inclined: Take a ride on the railroad between Portland, Oregon, and Tacoma, Washington, and note the conditions en route; or glance out of the car window as you ride through the timberland district in the Southern states—Alabama, Georgia, etc.

Oregon and Washington are bragging about what the native biped conceitedly calls enterprise, western spirit, progress, prosperity, etc. Poor fools! They imagine the so-called prosperity is due to the enterprise 54 or spirit of themselves, while any nature student could tell them that the business success of any territory is directly due to that territory's material that is marketed, and that as soon as the marketable material is used up the so-called enterprise, energy, spirit, etc., of the ego-marketman go up with it.

In Michigan (Bay City) thirty-five years ago the wasters used to boast that Bay City was going to outrival New York City in size, intellect, money wealth, social standing, etc., in a few years. All this on a little timber they were cutting and selling. It was remarked by a nature student that the success of their ambition depended upon the pine trees they were gradually consuming—ruthlessly cutting down to extermination—and a practical man suggested that they plant and propagate as well as cut and consume. Also it was

32

hinted that the lumber they made out of the trees was the only thing they had to make possible the social downfall of New York.

"Oh, by no means," they said; "we have enterprise and spirit; that's what counts."

But, the count was a failure—the trees giving out. Northern Michigan was turned into a sugar-beet farm, and most of the unfortunates who counted on making Bay City outrival New York are now of the very dust that nurtures the present-day material that their offspring exists upon.

The Michigan enterprise, spirit, etc., is now transferred to the few other timberland States, and the natives of to-day, the early day of plenty, are just like the old conceited Michiganders—they foolishly imagine the financial success of their territory is due to so-called personal energy, pride, enterprise, progress, etc., on the part of themselves, when any naturalist 55 knows that their prosperity is directly due to God's bountifulness—the abundance of marketable material—not man's effort or egotism.

When Oregon and Washington have lumbered all their timber the "enterprising" natives will not have rivaled New York socially or financially any more than the Michigander has accomplished this end; Oregon and Washington, without timber, like Michigan, will stay just where they are—if lucky enough not to go lower down in the social and financial standard—when their marketable material is exhausted.

Climate is a mere matter of pure air. What's the good in climate if it's smoked and burned? Any clean climate, hot or cold, is better than any soiled climate, hot or cold.

Marketable material, pure air, and pure water are the three big concerns of life; man isn't worthy of being included in the list of important things because he destroys these three mighty essentials. Material makes man more than man makes material.

Man's energy and egotism couldn't get a footing without marketable material. What the world needs is less of vain man and more plain market stuff.

Save the woods and waters.

56

CHAPTER IX

TROUT AND TROUTING

"A day with not too bright a beam;
A warm, but not a scorching, sun."
Charles Cotton

Where can I enjoy trout fishing amid good scenery and good cheer without its necessitating a lengthy absence from the city? That is a question which frequently rises in the mind of the toilers in the busy centers of the East, and it is one becoming daily more difficult to answer. Yet there are still nearby trout streams where a creel of from fifteen to fifty, or even more, in favorable weather, might be made. One such locality, which for years local sportsmen have proven, lies within a four hours' ride of either Philadelphia or New York. All that is necessary is to take the railroad, which conveys you to Cresco, in Monroe County, Pa., and a ride or drive of five miles through the Pocono Mountains will land you in the little village of Canadensis, in the valley of the Brodhead; and within the radius of a few miles on either side fully a dozen other unposted streams ripple along in their natural state, not boarded, bridged, dammed, or fenced by the hand of man, thanks to the naturally uncultivatable condition of the greater part of this paradise for trout fishers. The villagers of Canadensis 57 do their trading and receive their mail at Cresco, and it is an easy matter to obtain excellent food and lodgings for a dollar a day at one of the many farmhouses dotting here and there the valleys, and a seat when needful in one of the several private conveyances running every day between the two villages.

The open season for trout in Pennsylvania is from April 15th until July 15th, and there appears to be no particularly favored period during these three months, for the trout here afford sport equally well at all times, though they greatly vary in their tastes for the fly.

If the angler goes there in the early part of the open season, when the weather is cold, he should engage a room and take his meals at the farmhouse selected; but if the trip is made in the early part of June or any time after that, during the open season, camp life may be enjoyed with great comfort.

Two favorite waters within walking distance from any of the farmhouses in Canadensis are Stony Run and the Buckhill. The great Brodhead, a famous old water in the days of Thaddeus Norris, and noted then and now for its big trout, flows in the valley proper, within a stone's throw of the farmhouse at which I engaged quarters. Spruce Cabin Run, a mile distant, is a charming stream, but the trout here are not very large beyond the deep pools at the foot of Spruce Falls and in the water flowing through Turner's fields and woods above the falls.

Any of these streams will afford plenty of sport, but if one wishes to visit a still more wild, romantic, and beautiful trout water, he has only to walk a little farther or take a buckboard wagon and ride to the mighty Bushkill, a stream that must not be confounded 58 with the Buckhill, which lies in an opposite direction from Canadensis.

The Bushkill is the wildest stream in the region, and is fished less than any of the others named, one reason being that there are plenty of trout in the waters of Canadensis which can be fished without the Angler going so far. For those who like to camp, the Bushkill is the proper locality. I spent a day there with friends one season, and we caught in less than two hours, in the liveliest possible manner, all the trout five of us could eat throughout the day, and four dozen extra large ones which we took home to send to friends in the city.

"The trout in the Bushkill," remarked one of my companions, "are so wild that they're tame"—an expression based upon the greediness and utter disregard of the enemy with which fontinalis, in his unfamiliarity with man, took the fly. I remember having a number of rises within two feet of my legs as I was taking in my line for a front toss.

I know men who have many times traveled a thousand miles from New York on an angling trip to different famous waters who have not found either the sport or the scenery to be enjoyed on the Bushkill.

The lower Brodhead below the point at which this stream and Spruce Cabin Run come together is very beautiful. It is owned by a farmer who lives on its banks, and who has never been known to refuse Anglers permission to fish there when they asked for the privilege.

There are four natural features in the scenery about Canadensis that are especially prized by the countrymen there—the Sand Spring, Buckhill Falls, Spruce Cabin Falls, and the Bushkill Falls.

59

The Sand Spring is so called because grains of brilliant sand spring up with the water. This sand resembles a mixture of gold and silver dust; it forms in little clouds just under the water's bubble and then settles down to form and rise again and again. This effect, with the rich colors of wild pink roses, tiny yellow watercups, blue lilies, and three shades of green in the cresses and deer tongue that grow all about, produces a pretty picture. The spring is not over a foot in diameter, but the sand edges and the pool cover several feet. In drinking the water, strange to say, one does not take any sand with it.

Being located at one side of the old road between Cresco and Canadensis every visitor has an opportunity of seeing it without going more than a few feet out of his direct way. Some of the stories told about the old Sand Spring are worth hearing, and no one can tell them better or with more special pleasure than the farmers living thereabout. One man affirms that "more 'an a hundred b'ar and as many deer have been killed while drinking the crystal water of the spring."

Each of the falls is a picture of true wild scenery. Though some miles apart they may be here described in the same paragraph.

Great trees have fallen over the water from the banks and lodged on huge projecting moss-covered rocks; they are additional obstacles to the rushing, roaring, down-pouring water, which flows through and over them like melted silver. This against the dark background of the mountain woods, the blue and snow-white of the heavens, the green of the rhododendron-lined banks, and the streams' bottoms of all-colored stones creates a series of charming and ever-varying views.

60

A half dozen trout, weighing from one to two pounds and a half, may always be seen about the huge rock at the point where the lower Brodhead and the Spruce Cabin

Run come together, and hundreds may be seen in the stream below the Buckhill Falls. I do not know that fish may be actually seen in any other parts of the waters of Canadensis, but at these points the water is calm and the bottom smooth, and the specimens are plainly in view.

Do not waste time on the "flock" lying about the big rock at Brodhead Point. The trout there will deceive you. I played with them a half day, and before I began work on them I felt certain I would have them in my creel in a half-hour's time. They are a pack of pampered idlers who do not have to move a fin to feed. All the trout food comes rushing down both streams from behind these big rocks into the silent water and floats right up to the very noses of these gentlemen of leisure. If you have any practicing to do with the rod and fly do it here. These trout are very obliging; they will lie there all day and enjoy your casting all sorts of things at them. This is a good place to prove to yourself whether you are a patient fisherman or not.

And now a few words about the proper tackle for mountain streams. Most anglers use rods that are too heavy and too long. During my first visit I used a rod of eight feet, four ounces, and I soon found that, while it was a nice weight, it was too long for real convenience, although there were rods used there nine and ten feet long. My rod was the lightest and one of the shortest ever seen in the valley. There are only a few open spots where long casts are necessary, and a long, ordinary-weight trout rod is of very little 61 service compared with one of seven, seven and a half, or eight feet, four or three ounces, that can be handled well along the narrow, bush-lined, tree-branch-covered streams.

The greater part of the fishing is done by sneaking along under cover of the rocks, logs, bushes, and the low-hanging branches, as casts are made in every little pool and eddy. I use a lancewood rod, but of course the higher-priced popular split bamboo is just as good. I shall not claim my rod's material is the better of the two, as some men do when speaking of their tackle, but I am quite sure I shall never say the split bamboo is more than its equal. I do not advise as to the material; I speak only of the weight and length. Let every man use his choice, but I seriously advise him to avoid the cheap-priced split bamboo rod.

If split bamboo is the choice, let it be the work of a practical rod-maker. Any ordinary wood rod is better than the four-dollar split bamboo affair.

The leader should be of single gut, but the length should be a trifle more than is commonly used. Twelve feet is my favorite amount. The reel should be the lightest common click reel; the creel, a willow one that sells for a dollar in the stores; and the flies—here's the rub—must be the smallest and finest in the market. Large, cheap, coarse flies will never do for Eastern waters, and you must not fail to secure your list of the proper kind, as well as all your outfit, before you start on your trip. The only decent thing on sale in the village stores is tobacco.

When you buy your flies buy lots of them, for, be you a tyro or practical Angler, you will lose them easier on these streams than you imagine. Yes, you must be very careful about the selection of your flies. 62 They must be small and finely made, high-priced goods. I wish I might tell you who to have make them, but I dare not, lest I be charged with advertising a particular house. Regarding the patterns to use, I will say that none are more killing than the general list, if they are the best made and used according to the old rule all are familiar with—dark colors on cold days and bright ones on warm days. The later the season the louder the fly—that is, when the season closes during hot weather, as it does in Canadensis. My favorite time here is from June 15th to July 15th, the closing day, but any time after the first two weeks of the open season is very charming. I avoid the first week or two because the weather is then cold and the trout are more fond of natural bait than the artificial fly. Men take hundreds of fish early in the season with worms and minnows.

I never wear rubber boots to wade in. An old pair of heavy-soled shoes with spikes in their bottoms, and small slits cut in the sides to let the water in and out, and a pair of heavy woolen socks comprise my wading footwear. The slits must not be large enough to let in coarse sand and pebbles, but I find it absolutely necessary to have a slight opening, for if there be no means for the water to run freely in and out, the shoes fill from the tops and become heavy. Rubber boots are too hot for my feet and legs, while the water is never too cold. I have often had wet feet all day, and have never yet experienced any ill effects from it.

I never use a staff in wading, but I should, for here in some places it is very hard to wade. I have often fallen down in water up to my waist, overbalanced by the heavy current, where the bottoms were rough, with sharp, slimy stones. If you carry a staff, follow 63 the custom of the old Anglers and tie it to your body with a string to keep it out of the way and allow your hands to be as free as possible for a strike. Your landing-net should be a small one, minus any metal, with a foot and a half handle, and a string tied to a front button on your garment should allow it to be slung over your shoulder onto your back when not in use.

Of course, these little points about the use of different things are all familiar to the Angler with but the slightest experience, and will appear to him neither instructive nor interesting, but we must, as gentle Anglers, give a thought or two to the earnest tyro, for we were young once ourselves.

I always carry two fly-books with me; one big fellow with the general fly stock in, which is kept at the farmhouse, and a little one holding two dozen flies and a dozen leaders, which I carry on the stream. A string tied to this, too, will prevent the unpleasantness of having it fall in the water and glide away from you. I even tie a string to my pipe and knife. The outing hat is an important thing to me. Mine is always a soft brown or gray felt, and I use it to sit on in damp and hard places fifty times a day.

64

CHAPTER X

TROUTING IN CANADENSIS VALLEY

The Canadensis Valley in Monroe County, Pennsylvania, is a fontinalis paradise. With my friend George Blake I creeled the little heroes by the dozen every day for a week. We each could have easily caught fifty in an afternoon had we cared to do so, but there were other rural pleasures to attend to, and we were not dealing in fish, and saw more beauty in just enough to eat than in wasteful quantity. Fishermen are generally known as exaggerators, and I do not deny that they do sometimes resort to an innocent little fib when a yarn may amuse many and injure no one, but I must say that this region's beauties are too numerous to overpraise by all the exaggeration of all the fabricators in the world. No word of mouth or pen could do justice to nature in these mountains. And I need not elaborate on the fish; the truth is bold enough.

Brook trout weighing a quarter of a pound to a pound and a half are taken every day by Anglers, who more than fill their creels. Two gentlemen took in one day sixty-five beauties on the stream known as Stony Run, and two Philadelphia Anglers took half a hundred the day before above the Buckhill Falls. Another great stream in this region is the Bushkill, and still another is Brodhead's Creek. The latter 65 flows past our camp, and is famous for big trout. My favorite is Spruce Cabin Stream, above and below the beautiful Spruce Cabin Falls. There are big trout in this water, especially at the bottom of the falls, and I can—if I will—take fifty trout in an afternoon, and they'll weigh from a quarter of a pound to one pound and a half. I like something besides fish about a stream, and this is why I am fond of the Spruce Cabin water.

There are not many Anglers in love with the place. Though beautiful, it is very hard to fish. I have to creep under great trees that have fallen over the water and then wade up to my waist to gain certain points in order to get along down the stream. The banks are lined with trees and shrubbery, and my line is ever getting tangled. One does not need to be a fly-casting tournament Angler to fish any of the Canadensis waters. Distance in the cast is not required as much as accuracy at more than one or two places on each stream. The rest of the fishing is done by short, low casts, and by creeping under branches and letting the line float with the ripples into the eddies. Every step or two there are little falls, and in the white, bubbling water at their bottom a trout may be taken. Under the big fall, and in the still waters above and below, the big trout hide.

Artificial flies are the popular bait with the gentle Angler, though all sizes of trout will take worms, and the big, educated trout like minnows. Both small, medium, and large trout like flies if the flies are the right kind. We have had great trouble in getting good flies. I brought four dozen with me, and not over a half dozen of them are worth the snell tied to them; they are too clumsy in size, of coarse material, and 66 bad in color. The six decent ones are the work of an artist. I could give his name, but it might look like an advertisement and spoil my story. Trout like choice food just as much as human beings favor savory dishes. You may stick an oyster shell on a reed, and decoy a summer yellowleg, but you can't hook a trout on any kind of a fly. They know a thing or two.

Tyros who angle in a trout country without success go home and say there are no trout. They don't think about conditions of water and weather; about their line lighting in the water before their bait; about their coarse line and poor flies.

Trout are philosophers, not only the educated ones, those which have been hooked and seen others hooked, but trout in general. They're born that way. A young man came up here the other day with an old cane pole, weighing fully three pounds, and a big salt water sinker, and he went away saying there were few trout in these waters. I think he had a float with him, too, but am not sure.

A word or two about appropriate tackle for mountain streams, and I'll put up the pen and joint the rod again. In the city a few weeks ago I proudly displayed a four-ounce, nine-foot lancewood rod, and my friends laughed at me, saying it was too frail for any service. Now, I find this rod, shortened two feet, just the thing for this country where trout run small and where there's no long casting. I frequently run across good Anglers here with five-ounce rods, and have seen two four-ounce rods. There is no use for a rod above four ounces in weight and seven feet in length. When I come again I shall use a three-ounce rod. The reel should be the lightest and smallest common click, and the line the finest enameled silk,

Trout brook
THE TROUT BROOK

67

tapered if you like. The flies—here's the main thing—should be the best, and of the smallest brook trout pattern. Next year, when I make up my supply, I'll pack fully two hundred, and they'll be the dearest-priced flies, for they are none too good.

Oh, I must say a word about cooking and eating trout before I close. I've tried them in all styles, and the best way, I think, is when they're roasted over a camp fire on a little crotch stick, one prong in the head and the other in the tail. And the worst way, I think, is when they're fried in a pan with bad butter or poor lard.

Blake and I are in our glory. Our only displeasure is in knowing that our perspiring city friends are not as comfortable. The days here are warm and bright—not hot and close—and the nights cool and clear, so that we live merrily all the time.

I went a few hundred yards down the stream in front of the camp to two great bowlders, one morning, and there, during a little sun shower, took a Salvelinus fontinalis that weighed just a little over two pounds and a quarter. He rose to a pinkish, cream-colored fly, with little brown spots on the wings. I forget its name, but it's one of the six really good ones I referred to. I decided to keep the large captive alive, so I took off one of the cords tied about my trousers at the bottoms (I never wear wading boots in warm weather), put it through his gill, and tied the other end to a submerged tree-root. Later, Mr. Trout was lodged in a small box, with bars tacked over the top, and placed under a spout running from an old mill race. He was a big specimen—large enough to saddle and ride to town, the cook said. And pretty—as pretty as a gathering of lilacs and giant ferns decked with wintergreen berries.

68

CHAPTER XI

THE TROUTER'S OUTFIT

The rod for stream fishing should weigh from three to six ounces and measure in length from seven to nine feet. Split bamboo and lancewood are two of the best rod materials. If you cannot afford a good split bamboo do not buy a cheap one; choose a lancewood.

The line should be a small-sized waterproofed silk one. The reel, a small common light rubber click, holding twenty-five or thirty-five yards.

The landing net, used to take the fish from the water after being hooked, should be made of cane with linen netting, and have no metal about it. The handle should be about a foot long. Tie a string to the handle, tie the string to a button on your coat under your chin, and then toss the net over your back out of the way.

The creel, or fish basket, should be a willow one about the size of a small hand satchel. This should have a leather strap, to be slung over the right shoulder, allowing the creel to rest on the left hip.

The hat should be a soft brown or gray felt with two-inch brim. This may be used as a cushion to sit down upon on rocks or in damp places.

The footwear may be either rubber boots, leather shoes, or rubber wading trousers. If the water is warm, wear leather shoes, and have nails put in the 69 thick soles to keep your feet from slipping in swift water and on slimy stones. If you choose rubber boots see that they are of the light, thin, thigh-fitting sort and not the clumsy affairs with straps attached.

The fly-book for use on the stream should have room for not more than a dozen flies, with pockets for leaders, silk cord, small shears, and other tools. A larger book for your general stock of flies and leaders may be left at your rural lodgings with your tackle box and other traps.

The leader, to which are attached the flies in use, should be of the finest quality of single silk gut, and in length three feet. Two of these attached make a cast, though I prefer a longer cast of leader.

The coat and general clothing should be of a dead-grass, gray, or light brown color. Have plenty of pockets, and tie a string to nearly everything you carry in them, so you cannot lose them if they fall from your hands.

The flies—every known variety of trout fly, providing you order these of the finest make.

Do not undertake to go trouting stintingly equipped, which is not saying that you are to dress and act like a circus clown. But you must be properly outfitted. Good carpenters make good houses, but their work is better and more pleasant if they have good tools.

The tyro who is not fortunate enough to have the friendship of a practical fisherman to whom he may apply for advice should read the works on angling and ichthyology by Izaak Walton, Henry William Herbert ("Frank Forester"), Seth Green, Charles Hallock. Wm. C. Harris, Thaddeus Norris, Genio C. Scott. Frederick Mather, Robert Roosevelt, G. Brown Goode, Kit Clarke, Dr. Jas. A. Henshall, Charles 70 Zibeon Southard, Dr. Edward Breck, Emlyn M. Gill. George M. L. LaBranche, Louis Rhead, Eugene McCarthy, Dr. Henry van Dyke, David Starr Jordan. Dr. Evermann, Prof. Baird, Tarlton H. Bean, Richard Marston, Frederick E. Pond ("Will Wildwood"). Mary Orvis Marbury, A. Nelson Cheney, Charles F. Orvis, Dr. Charles Frederick Holder, Perry D. Frazer. Emerson Hough, Rowland E. Robinson, Isaac McLellan. Francis Endicott, Dean Sage, Wm. C. Prime. Henry P. Wells, Judge Northrup, John Harrington Keene, et al., and make a study of the catalogues of the better class of sporting-goods houses.

71

CHAPTER XII

TROUT FLIES, ARTIFICIAL AND NATURAL

"The wide range of difference between the wet fly and the dry fly lies in the fact that the wet fly is an imitation of no special thing active and living, while the dry fly purports to be an imitation of the natural fly. It is generally a well-known fact that any of our well-known American wet flies can be converted into exceptionally good dry flies by giving them an ablution of oil."—Robert Page Lincoln, Outdoor Life. September, 1915.

Then the wet fly resembles the dry fly, and therefore the wet fly is an imitation of the living fly. Of course it is. Is not the artificial black gnat imitative of the live black gnat? And is not the white miller artificial fly patterned after the living white miller fly? Certainly. Mary Orvis Marbury, author of Favorite Flies, and daughter of Charles F. Orvis, one of America's greatest fly-makers, says so. So says William C. Harris, Seth Green, Frank Forester, Louis Rhead, A. Nelson Cheney, Frederick Mather, Dr. Henshall, Charles Hallock, Dean Sage, William C. Prime, Charles Z. Southard, Dr. van Dyke, Edward Breck, et al.

All angling writers in discoursing upon artificial flies use the expressions "in season," "seasonable flies," etc. Now, how could this or that artificial fly be in 72 season if it were not copied from the living fly? Of course, there are some artificial flies that are not copied from nature, but the artificial fly in general is a duplicate of the living thing. "When a fly is said to be in season," says Alfred Ronalds, "it does not follow that it is abroad on every day of its existence." But, our opinions must not be harshly expressed—rather set forth

41

"in pleasant discourse," as Walton says—for, as Pritt tells us, "one of the charms of angling is that it presents an endless field for argument, speculation, and experiment."

After the foregoing excerpt and my comment upon it appeared in the New York Press (Sept. 11, 1915). I wrote several of the authorities mentioned, asking their views on the subject, and following will be found their replies.

Henry van Dyke, author of Little Rivers, Days Off, Fisherman's Luck, etc.:

For flies as "wet," or flies as "dry."
I do not care a whit—not I!
The natural fly is dry, no doubt.
While through the air he flits about;
But, lighting on the stream, you bet
He very often gets quite wet.
This fact is known to all the fish;
They take their flies just as they wish.
Upon the surface or below.
Precisely why we do not know.
The honest Angler should not be
A man of rigid theory.
But use the most alluring fly.
And sometimes "wet," and sometimes "dry."

Louis Rhead, author of The Book of Fish and Fishing: "After thirty-two years' active fishing for trout, beginning with a worm as a bait, I have developed 73 through various stages to know fish with nothing but my own nature flies. I have made careful color pictures of all the most abundant insects and produced flies tied to exactly imitate them. Many insects do not and cannot float, yet an imitation can be made of them to fish wet. The English dry fly is not of necessity a copy of the natural insect. Halford has many fancy dry flies that are not copies of insects. Nearly all American commercial trout flies are fancy flies, and do not imitate insects. To be exact, in fishing with a floating fly it is only right to use copies of insects that will float, mostly drakes. The average Angler has been sadly fooled by this so-called dry-fly fishing, and books have been written (mostly culled from British sources), making Anglers more bewildered than ever."

Charles Zibeon Southard, author of Trout Fly-Fishing in America: "In reply to your question about trout flies, 'Am I right?' I would say that unquestionably you are. From the earliest days of trout fly-fishing it has been the intention of Anglers to have their flies resemble as far as possible the natural ones found upon their trout waters. One has only to read dear old Izaak Walton and the many noted fly-fishing authorities that have followed to the present day to be convinced of your view. Of course the art of fly-tying has advanced with mighty strides during the past fifteen years and more especially during the past ten years, and to the makers of 'dry' flies for the wonderful development of the artificial fly too much credit, in my judgment, cannot be given. That wet flies are not such remarkable imitations of the natural flies as are the dry flies goes almost without saying. As a matter of fact it is not the question 74 which fly is the better imitation, but that both the wet fly and the dry fly are patterned, in most cases, after the natural flies. From the time of Walton and before that, wet flies have been patterned after natural flies. In many instances nowadays wet flies are not designed to represent natural flies, but such flies are freaks, are short-lived, and are seldom used by real trout fly-fishermen. There is no doubt in my mind that taken as a whole wet flies have been intended to represent natural flies, but quite often in the past and in the present day have not been and are not good imitations. As the art of fly-tying has advanced, more nearly do the artificial represent the natural flies, and this advancement is due, in a great measure, to the makers of dry flies. Speaking from a practical standpoint, the so-called dry flies are the very best wet flies obtainable, and on most American trout waters more trout will be caught on them when fished wet than when fished dry, especially the fontinalis. "

Dr. James A. Henshall, author of The Book of the Black Bass: "Regarding the 'Trout Flies' clipping sent me for comment I think the mention of my name in it is sufficient without adding anything more."

Dr. Edward Breck, author of The Way of the Woods, etc.: "I suppose that I may subscribe to your paragraph in answer to Mr. Lincoln. We old chaps all know that laying down any hard and fast rules for trout is a futile undertaking; there are so many exceptions, and les extrêmes se touchent so very often. Many wet flies are certainly not imitations of natural flies nor are they meant to be; as, for example, the Parmachenee belle, which they say Wells fashioned to imitate the belly-fin of a trout, always known to be a killing lure. 'Non-university' trout grab anything 75 that looks like food, whether it has the appearance of an insect or something else. The more educated fish of the more southern waters may make finer distinctions. It is a vast subject, and as many authorities may be found for almost any statement as for the several pronunciations of the word 'Byzantine.' You remember the scoffing English Angler who dyed his dry flies blue and red and took a lot of fish with them, to the scandal of the purists! The charm of the whole thing is precisely that there are no rules. It is like style in writing English. Every man makes his own. Whether it is more pleasing in the sight of Saint Izaak to wait for a fish to begin feeding before casting over him, or for a man to sally forth, and, by dint of knowledge and patience and skill, actually make the trout rise to his lure, what arrogant mortal shall judge?"

Robert Page Lincoln: "Perhaps I should have said some wet flies are an imitation of no special object connected with living things. In the list of wet flies there are experimentations galore that will serve as well as any of the standard regulation flies. I can sit down and construct offhand a fly to be used as wet or submerged that I feel sure I can use with as much success as with the miller, gnat, or any other fly that is no doubt much on the order of an imitation of the natural. Perhaps in writing the article I was thinking too deeply of the eccentric nondescripts that do not imitate nature. Yet these nondescripts (flies tied anyway to suit the fancy), yet having hackle wings, etc., will get the fish; they are drawn in the water gently back and forth, thus purporting to be some insect drowning; yet I doubt very much if the fish can tell what sort of a fly, living fly, it should be. I 76 do not care; it is the motion, the apparent endeavor of the fly to get out of that watery prison that arouses the fish's blood. However, Halford says: 'The modern theory is that these patterns (the wet flies) are taken by the fish for the nymphæ or pupæ—these being the scientific names of the immature insects at the stage immediately preceding the winged form.... Candidly, however, the presence of the wings in the sunk fly pattern has puzzled me, because in my experience I have never seen the winged insects submerged by the action of the stream. Sedges do at times descend to oviposit and so do certain spinners, but the appearance under this condition, with an air bubble between their wings, resembles nothing so much as a globe of mercury—an appearance which bears no resemblance to the ordinary sunk fly patterns.' I have been strictly a devotee to the wet-fly form, and always hold that it is the better fly for our swift Western streams; in the wet form certainly it is the better fly two thirds of the time. Still, glassy pools, even smooth waters, come few and far between, but, where they are, there the dry fly is a valuable addition to the Angler's outfit. You might change my article (in the paragraph in question) to read thus: 'The wide range of difference between some wet flies and the dry fly lies in the fact that a good number of wet flies are an imitation of no special thing active and living, while the majority of the dry flies purport to be an imitation of natural flies.' This would exclude the wet flies that make good dry flies, namely the suggested millers, gnats, etc. It would be interesting to know the number of captures made with wet flies as they fall lightly to water and for a moment ride the brim. Captures have been made wherein two thirds 77 of the time the wet fly has lain on the surface but a scant moment before it was seized. In my great number of articles printed in the universal outdoor press I have always suggested that the fly be cast easily to water, expecting, first, a rise as it lies on the surface; second, failing at this, then the fly submerges and is drawn in the water, to assure the opening and closing of hackles, thus purporting to imitate the drowning, struggling insect."

Charles Hallock, author of The Sportsman's Gazetteer, The Salmon Fisher, etc.: "I have nothing more to say. I hung up my trout rod last summer at Chesterfield. Mass., in my eighty-second year. So, my fly-book is closed. Let younger Anglers do the talking and discuss ad infinitum. Flies are not on my line. Good-bye."

"To frame the little animal
Let nature guide thee."
—Gay.
TROUT TAKING THE FLY

"You will observe when casting the wet fly ... that trout seldom rise to the fly when it first strikes the water ... after years of experience I am prepared to state as my opinion that such a thing does not happen once in thirty casts."—Charles Zibeon Southard, Trout Fly-Fishing in America.

This has not been my experience with fontinalis in the streams and ponds of Long Island, N. Y., and the mountain brooks of Pennsylvania, where many of my trout took the fly almost before it touched the water. I have seen trout catch large live flies in the air a few inches over the surface. I think large trout in clear, still ponds easily see the cast fly before it 78 alights. The trout in rapid streams may not be so alert, but I have certainly caught many a specimen on the fly the instant the lure touched the water.

Mr. William M. Carey, who is responsible for the frontispiece in this volume, is positive trout often jump out of the water in taking the fly. I, too, have seen trout do so. It is not a regular practice of the species, but I easily recall many instances of the trout leaping clear of the surface and taking the fly in the descent. Trout of all sizes will often strike both living and artificial flies with their tails, this either in play or to disable the insect. A writer in Forest and Stream (January 9, 1901) says: "In fishing a trout stream in northern Michigan I was using a cast of a Parmachenee belle and a brown hackle. I was wading downstream, and I came to a place where a tree had fallen into the stream, and after several casts I noticed some small trout following my flies. I cast again, and while my flies were five or six inches from the water a trout four or five inches long jumped clear out of the water, grabbed my Parmachenee belle and immediately dove with it in its mouth. I believe the same trout did the same thing several times while I was fishing there. These were brook trout and they were not jumping except when they jumped at my flies."

The foregoing comments were submitted to Mr. Southard, and he writes me:

"What you say about catching trout in Long Island waters and the mountain brooks of Pennsylvania is entirely true. During the early spring season I have caught, at times, many small trout on such waters in precisely the same way, and in addition there have been days on many different waters where occasionally during the whole of the open season I have caught 79 trout when they rose the moment the fly alighted upon the water. These experiences of ours alone, however, do not establish as a fact nor as a general proposition that trout rise to a fly more often when it first alights upon the water than after the fly has been fished or played by the Angler; nor that my statement as a general proposition is not a correct one.

"The statement was perhaps poorly worded and thus misleading, and I should have said that on an average trout do not rise to a fly once in thirty casts when it first alights upon the water. My opinion was based, first, upon trout fly-fishing on all kinds of fishable waters wherever found; second, upon all sizes of trout from the minimum of six inches to the maximum of thirty inches whether or not they were indigenous or planted fish; third, upon my own experience of over twenty-five years as well as the opinion of many Anglers and guides with an experience covering a longer period than my own; fourth, upon my knowledge of the habits and habitats of trout under the many varying conditions which govern their lives and actions.

"Unfortunately most Anglers have given almost no thought to studying and analyzing 'the art of fly-fishing' to the end that they may become better and more successful fishermen and thus enjoy to a greater extent the pleasures of the clean, dignified, and delightful sport of angling. It is not surprising then that an Angler upon first thought, even an experienced one, might think that trout rise to flies when they first alight upon the water more often than once in thirty casts because he remembers only the rises and his successes, but pays very little attention to the lack of either. How many Anglers know approximately the number of casts they make in an hour? How 80 many know the number of rises they have and when? How many know the number of trout that rise and strike and are hooked and landed? The answer is 'Few indeed'; and those who hazard a guess are usually far from the facts.

"The average fly-fishing Angler casts his fly or flies, on most waters, from five to seven times a minute and the less experienced Angler from seven to ten times. With the more experienced Angler this means that he casts from 300 to 420 times in an hour and in five hours from 1500 to 2100 times. Let us take the lesser number as a basis of reasoning; in one hour, if once in thirty casts a trout rose, struck, and was hooked when the fly first alighted upon the water, the Angler's creel would be richer by ten fish and in five hours by fifty fish. Then to this number should be added the trout that rise, strike, and are hooked after the fly has alighted upon the water and has been fished or played by the Angler. Would it not be a fair proposition to say that at least as many trout would be caught under the latter circumstances as the former? To my mind it would. The Angler then would have creeled one hundred fish in five hours. As some trout, even with the most expert of Anglers, are bound to be lost let us be liberal and place the loss at fifty per cent., thus making the Angler's net catch fifty instead of one hundred fish. Think this over and think over what your experience has been, day after day and season after season, and ask yourself if a catch of this size is not very unusual on the best of trout fishing waters. So far as my own experience goes it certainly is most unusual, and I fish on many fine waters each year and for at least one hundred days.

81

"There are some places, especially in the State of Maine, and notably 'The Meadow Grounds' of 'The Seven Ponds,' Franklin County, where at times large numbers of small trout, running from five to seven or eight inches, can be caught in a fishing day of five hours and I have known of Anglers catching, though not killing, from three hundred to seven hundred trout and most of them rose to the flies when they first alighted upon the water. At 'Tim Pond,' Maine, the only place I know where more trout can be caught on the fly than by bait, one hundred to two hundred trout have been caught in one day on the fly, but in most instances these trout take the fly not when it alights upon the water but after it has been played. Such occurrences as these, however, take place where countless numbers of small trout are found in the shallow waters of remarkable and wonderful natural breeding and propagating sections. Instances of this kind prove nothing because they are the great exception and the art of fly-fishing is not brought into play, for one fly is as good as another and the small boy with his fifty-cent pole can catch just as many trout as the man of experience with his thirty-dollar rod of split bamboo. Yet in expressing my opinion about trout rising to a fly when it first alights upon the water I took into consideration just such instances as I have cited.

"'For your own satisfaction and education,' to quote from my book, 'when the opportunity offers, keep an account of the number of rises you get when your fly first strikes the water and the number you get after you have begun to fish the fly, and so prove for yourself what the real facts are on this subject.'

"It is unquestionably true that all trout both large 82 and small, when in clear, still water that is shallow, easily see a cast fly before it alights upon the surface.

"At times, under certain conditions both on streams and lakes, trout will leap into the air and take small as well as large flies in the air. But seldom will large or very large trout rise above the surface for any kind of fly either real or artificial.

"In order that there may be no misunderstanding I would say that I classify the size of trout as follows:

"Small trout, 8 inches and under.

"Medium sized trout, 9 to 13 inches.

"Large trout, 14 to 18 inches.

46

"Very large trout, 19 inches and over.

"Trout found in rapid streams are more alert than trout found elsewhere; they in most cases represent the perfection of trout life in all its different phases. Trout in rapid streams are snappy risers to both the real and artificial fly but owing to the current they frequently 'fall short' and fail to strike and take the fly. Such trout when they do take the fly are the easiest to hook because they often hook or help to hook themselves owing to the current.

"Your experience can hardly be said to differ materially from my own in the instances you mention, but I cannot help thinking that you have failed to take into account the many times when you have returned with an empty or very nearly empty creel or to consider the number of times you have actually cast your fly on the days when the creel was full to overflowing.

"If you have cited your usual experience then I heartily congratulate you upon your skill and upon your good fortune in knowing such remarkable fishing waters wherein there dwells 'the most beautiful fish that swims.'"

83

I fully agree with Mr. Southard, and I, too, should have worded my comment differently, though I didn't declare, fortunately, that most of my trout were taken the instant the fly touched the water. I used the word "many" in both instances where I spoke of the trout taking the fly. I think I should have considered more deeply Mr. Southard's line "once in thirty casts"; then we'd have understood each other. However, no crime has been committed; far from it, for look you, reader, what you have gained—all this delightful extra practical reading; and remember ye, "one of the charms of angling," as Pritt says, "is that it presents an endless field for argument, speculation, and experiment."

84

CHAPTER XIII

THE BROOK TROUT'S RIVAL

When the German brown trout was introduced in the brook trout streams of Pennsylvania some years ago fly-fishermen condemned the act because they believed the brook trout (S. fontinalis) was superior to the brown trout as a game fish. Deforestation, rendering the streams too warm for the brook trout, has changed the fly-fisherman's feeling in the matter. The brown trout can thrive in warm water, and with the brook trout's gradual extermination the brown trout is being welcomed as the next best thing. A correspondent at Reading, Pa., signing himself "Mourner"—he mourns the passing of the true brook trout—declares the brown trout strikes harder than the brook trout and after being hooked, unlike the brook trout, makes two or three leaps out of the water, but is not so gamey and cunning as the brook trout and tires out much quicker. The German species has been popular because it attains a larger size quickly and destroys almost every fish in the streams, including the brook trout. "The fly-fishermen who for years have matched their skill, cunning, artifice, and prowess against the genuine brook trout that since creation dawned have inhabited the mountain brooks that flow down every ravine," says Mourner, "have had forced on them, as never before, the sad truth 85 that, like the deer, bear, quail, woodcock, and grouse, brook trout are slowly but surely passing. There never was a fish so gamy, elusive, and eccentric, so beautiful and so hard to deceive and capture by scientific methods as the native brook trout. No orator has yet risen to fully sound its praises; no poet to sing its merits as they deserve; no painter to produce its varied hues. The brook trout was planted in the crystal waters by the Creator 'when the morning stars sang together' and fontinalis was undisturbed, save as some elk, deer, bear, panther, or wildcat forded the shallows of his abode, or some Indian or mink needed him for food. In this environment the brook trout grew and thrived. Much warfare made him shy and suspicious until he became crafty to a degree. The brook trout successfully combated man's inventive genius in the shape of agile rods, artificial flies and other bait calculated to fool the most wary, and automatic reels, landing nets, and other paraphernalia designed to rob a game fish of 'life, liberty, and the pursuit of happiness.' But it was not until the tanner and acid factory despoiler turned poisoned refuse into the streams and the dynamiter came upon the scene and the sheltering trees were cut away by the lumberman, letting in the sun and warming the water to a nauseous tepidity, that the brave trout faltered, hesitated, and then quit the uneven conquest. Carp and bass were planted in the streams to further endanger the brook trout's existence. Next the California trout and the German brown trout, who prey upon the true brook trout's progeny, followed, till finally, beaten, baffled, dismayed, poisoned, routed, and overwhelmed by the superior numbers and size of a cannibalistic race, he gradually began his 86 retreat. It is good-bye to the brook trout now. With him it was either cool pools, solitude, and freedom, or extermination. The waters that pour down into larger streams are sad memories now of his school playgrounds. No more will the sportsman's honest hunger be appeased by the brook trout's fine-grained flesh from hardening waters of nearby mountain brooks. But memory of the brook trout cannot be wrested from those who knew him at his best, and braved personal danger from rattler, bear, and wildcat to win him from the crystal waters. The brook trout has been butchered to make a carp's holiday. Gone he may be now, but he will live forever in the dreams of all true fishermen as the real aristocrat of the mountain streams. The like of him will not soon be seen again." The Fish Commission has mastered the science of the artificial propagation of the brook trout—millions are now produced with little trouble and expense—and the stocking of waters is a common practice, but the Fish Commission can't propagate forests and woodland streams. Mourner must know that the brook trout itself is not hard to save; it is the preservation of its wild habitat that is the great puzzle. If the United States Forestry Department will protect the trout streams from the greedy lumberman, the factoryman, and acid maker, the Fish Commission will have no trouble in saving the brook trout.

87

CHAPTER XIV

Most women who indulge in fishing are, like children, mere fish takers, not Anglers, but the craft is honored by the association of many fine female devotees who study and practice the gentle art in its fullest meaning—a devotion to the poetic, artistic, healthful, and humane elements in piscatorial pursuits. Dame Juliana Berners, who wrote the earliest volume on gentle fishing (1500), was the first celebrated example of the artful and merciful woman fisher, and Cleopatra the first female to make notorious the coarse and ungodly method in fishing for pastime. Sweet Dame Berners believed in angling—the desire of fair treatment to the quarry, correct tackle, a love of the pursuit superior to greed for number in the catch, and a heavenly admiration of the general beauties of nature in the day as well as in the play; and brutal Cleopatra believed in mere fishing, the killing of the greatest number, regardless of means, mercy, or method.

Our modern Dame Bernerses and Cleopatras in the fishing fold are many. The wife who aids the net fisherman—the marine farmer whose calling emulates the professional duties of Jesus' disciples, Peter. Andrew, James, and John—does not count. Her part in fishing, while by no means angling, is as honest as the work of the upland farmer's helpmate, and God 88 Himself will not condemn little children, male or female, who fish indiscriminately, "because they do not know." Fishing for the modern market is just as honorable as market fishing was in the ancient days when Jesus praised the net fishermen and made them His nearest and dearest friends, and angling—merciful ungreedy fishing with humane tackle and a clear conscience—is even more righteous than net fishing, because, while the main result of the Angler's pursuit is the same as the marketman's— fish taking—the Angler's method of capture is far less cruel, and his creel of fish is far less in number than the boatful of the marketman.

The distinction in angling and fishing is made by the modes employed in the taking, the killing, and the disposing of the fishes. Any fisherman who uses tackle appropriate to the various species, who is not greedy in his catch, who plays his game with mercy, who dispatches it with the least suffering, who disposes of it without wanton waste, and who is thankful to the Maker for the ways and means for all these conditions, is an Angler. And cannot woman be as artful and gentle in pursuits and as appreciative in feeling as man? Surely. England and Scotland and Ireland are famous for their women Anglers, and Maine, the Adirondacks, California, and Canada boast of the finest female fly-casters in the world. There are more women Anglers in these last-named territories than there are men Anglers in all other parts of the United States. A woman, Mary Orris Marbury, wrote the best volume scientifically descriptive of trout, bass, and salmon flies of modern times, and Cornelia Crosby, a daughter of the Maine wilderness, is the fly-fishing enthusiast of America.

89

Great minds, male and female, have gentle hearts. Izaak Walton handled a frog as if he loved him. Cowper would not unnecessarily hurt a worm. Lincoln upset his White House Cabinet to rescue a mother pig from a mire. Webster neglected the Supreme Court to replace a baby robin that had fallen from its nest. Moses, John the Divine, Washington, Thoreau. Audubon, Wilson, and even Napoleon and Cæsar the mighty mankillers were all of tender hearts, and all of these were—Anglers. Christ was only a fisher of men, but He loved and associated with the fishers of fishes. Walton, the father of fishers and fishing, angled for the habits of fishes more than for their hides. The capture of a fish was insignificantly incidental to the main notion of his hours abroad—his divine love of the waters, the fields, the meadows, the skies, the trees, and God's beautiful things that inhabit these. 'Tis the soul we seek to replenish, not the creel. So a Long Island dairyman's daughter views the theme, and she handles the mother and baby trout as if she loved them. Salvelinus fontinalis, little salmon of the streams, the Angler's dearly beloved brook trout—this is the dairymaid's special delight. She breeds these rainbow-hued beauties and broods over them, she feeds and fondles them, and they are to her what David's holy, fleecy flock were to him—his blessed charge by heavenly day and cardinal care at night. They feed from her hand, and play like kittens with her fingers. Cleopatra cleaved her fishes with a murderous hand and hook. Audrey cuddles her trout with a magnanimous mind and heart.

The trout, with all its famous beauty of color, grace, and outline, all its army of admirers, all the glory of its aqua-fairyland habitat, all its seeming gentility of 90 breeding and character, is none the less a little villain at the killing game, like the less admired feline and canine and serpentine species, for he will devour the daintiest and gaudiest butterfly that ever poet sang of. Fledgling robins and bluebirds, orioles and wrens are meat and drink to him. Young chipmunks and squirrels that lose their balance in the storm fall into his ready maw. The bat, the bee, the beetle and ladybug are rich morsels to his gastric eye, and the golden lizard, the umber ant, the silvery eel, the crawling angleworm, the chirping cricket, creeping spider, the grasshopper, the hopping frog, and e'en the heavenly hummingbird are but mealtime mites to him. Perhaps the knowledge of this life-destroying trait in all the fishes made Cleopatra indifferent to the gentler mode of fishing, just as it had a softer influence over Audrey, for she, though loving both the fishes and their victims, was induced to angle and thus punish, but never kill, her finny favorites. She had heard of the artificial dry fly Anglers of Europe using the barbless hook that held the trout without pain or injury, and this she made herself, tying up dozens of somber-hued and lustrous patterns on the bent bit of bronze that formed the snare. The ruly trout who gently waver in the deep pool, satisfied with the food supplied by their fair mistress, and who behave themselves when they swim abroad in the general ponds and streams, are not molested, but the rebellious urchins who, disdaining the bits of liver and worm fed to them in plenty, go forth to slay the happy ladybug and butterfly, are made the game of the barbless hook.

Audrey has five or six thousand trout in the pond and the stream flowing into it. The surrounding country is wildly beautiful, the water being surrounded 91 by great trees of elm, hickory, maple, beech, chestnut, walnut, and dogwood, under which is spread a rich green lawn, with here and there patches of wild shrubs, vines, and ground flowers. Rustic benches circle the water-edge oaks, and sleek deer, as tame as Belgian hares, browse on the rich grass and eat dainty morsels from the palms of their human friends. Cleopatra's marble perch basin was cold and deadly in its artificial atmosphere. Audrey's woodland trout preserve is warm and lifelike in its natural loveliness.

92

CHAPTER XV

THE BROOK TROUT INCOGNITO

(The "Sea Trout")

I am the wiser in respect to all knowledge and the better qualified for all fortunes for knowing that there is a minnow in that brook."—Thoreau.

There is still considerable argument about the identification and classification of the sea trout. Some authorities still claim the sea trout is a distinct species; others declare it to be the brook trout, Salvelinus fontinalis, that goes to sea from the fresh water ponds and streams.

The squeteague (vulgo weakfish, wheatfish, sea bass, white sea bass, carvina, checutts, shecutts, yellowfin, drummer, bluefish, squit, suckermang, succoteague, squitee, chickwit, gray trout, sun trout, salmon, salmon trout, shad trout, sea trout, salt-water trout, spotted trout, etc.) is not a trout of any sort; so this species need not be considered in this sea trout discussion.

My personal theory concerning the sea trout is that any trout that goes to sea is a sea trout, and that more than one species of trout go to sea—whenever they have the opportunity.

The small-stream trout that visit the ocean do so 93 mainly in search of a change in food; the sea-going trout of large rivers are impelled to leave their fresh water retreats for the ocean waters also to satisfy a desire for new varieties of food, but more so because of an instinct that warns them of the danger of remaining in the fresh-water rivers during certain periods of the year—the coldest seasons when the waters freeze to the river bottom, and in the melting time, when the ice thaws into huge sharp-edge chunks, and the mass of ice, swift-running water, and rocks turn the rivers into raging, roaring floods that would cut and bruise the trout unmercifully.

Nature makes these large-river brook trout in the calm periods of spring, summer, and autumn, and sea trout in severe winter weather and during dangerous flood time.

The broad streams of the west coast of Newfoundland—Fishels River, Crabs River, Big and Little Codroy Rivers, Big and Little Barachois Rivers, and Robinson's River—afford the best evidence of trout migrating to the sea to escape the fury of the flood, and any of the little trout streams in any part of the world where the streams flow into salt water will afford the student means of observing the trout's fondness for marine excursions in search of a change of diet.

Just as the different species of trout are widely contrasting in colors, shapes, sizes, traits, etc., while in their natural habitat—fresh water—so are they confoundingly different in these matters while sojourning in salt water.

The true brook trout (Salvelinus fontinalis) is of various shades, shapes and sizes, these depending upon the character of the water he inhabits. In shallow, swift streams of a light color pebble bottom 94 the specimens in general are likely to be thin, narrow, and of a bright gray hue, though, of course, there are individual specimens in this condition of water that are exceptions to the rule—a few old specimens who have sheltered themselves for years in dark, deep, steady spots under the protruding bank of the stream, or along the side of a sunken tree stump, etc. This autocrat of the eddy is fat, stocky, and dark in color, just the opposite of his younger relatives of the swift-running part of the stream.

The brook trout of deep, still dark-bottom ponds are fatter, darker, broader, of duller color and of slower motion than their brothers of the rapid waters. The trout's shape, weight, size, and color are influenced by its food, its age, its activity, its habitat, and its habits. Its color corresponds to the color of the water bottom, and will change as the water bottom changes. If removed to a new water, where the bottom color is different from the bottom color of its first abode—lighter or darker, as the case may be—it will gradually grow to a corresponding shade, blending with its new habitat just as its colors suited the stones and grasses and earthy materials of its native domain.

The landlocked trout, if imprisoned in a deep, dark, muddy-bottom, shaded woodland pool, will be dull in color, stocky in shape, and of sluggish habits. The trout confined to a bubbling fountain pool, with a bottom of golden sand, at the foot of a waterfall, in the full glare of the sun, will be of albino character.

Perhaps no other fish offers specimens of its own kind so deeply in contrast as fontinalis. This is scientifically and interestingly illustrated in many ways—color, size, shape, form, action, environment, etc. For example, consider the big, fat, long, strong, 95 copper-color brook trout that, having access to salt water, gormandizes upon the multitudinous food of the sea—shrimp, killifish, spearing, spawn, crab, etc.—and the tiny, active, silvery albinolike brook trout that is locked in a small foamy basin under a dashing waterfall, feeding only upon minute crustacea and the insect life that is carried to its watery prison. These two specimens are not freakish individuals of their species—like the blunt-nose specimen and the various other deformities—but are quite common contrasting representatives of their tribe.

If we were to display in a group side by side one of each of the shape-and-color-differing specimens—one large copper-shade, sea-going brook trout, one tiny silvery, fountain-locked brook trout, one ordinary-environed brook trout, one blunt-nose brook trout, etc.—the fact of their being of an identical species would be correctly appreciated by the scientific man only.

I am not resorting to poetic license or theorizing or delving into ancient precedents to carry my point of natural history, for I once captured one of the big, sea-going specimens, and my friend, James Cornell, angling in an adjacent stream the same day, brought to creel a little silvery beauty of the foamy waterfall. Shape, form, tint, weight—every mood and trait—were of astounding contrast in these two specimens, yet both were of the same species, the true brook trout; my dark, strenuous three-pounder taken in the open, brackish creek as I cast from the salt meadowland sod banks, and Cornell's albinolike gamester succumbing to the fly in the foamy fountain of a deep woodland brook; both specimens widely separated in appearance, habits, and habitat, but still both legitimate 96 brothers of the family fontinalis—little salmon of the streams.

Trout in the sea feed on shrimp, the spawn of herring, and on the entrails of cod and other species of fishes thrown away by market fishermen.

If the sea-going trout did not eat the spawn of the herring, herring would be too plentiful for Nature's even-distribution arrangement. The sea trout is gorged with herring spawn, which lies in heaps like so much sawdust on the shores and shallow places of the ocean. Cod spawn and milt float on the water's surface; the spawn of the herring sinks.

The sea trout fresh from the streams is plump, has bright red spots, and is in ordinary color when it goes to sea; when it returns to the streams, though bigger (longer) and stronger, it is comparatively thin, and is of white or silver-sheened shade.

Prof. George Brown Goode (American Fishes): "The identity of the Canadian sea trout and the brook trout is still denied by many, though the decision of competent authorities has settled the question beyond doubt."

Eugene McCarthy (Familiar Fish): "Many Anglers are now turning their attention to catching sea trout, either on account of the novelty of the sport or because they believe that they are taking a new variety of fish. That there is novelty in such fishing cannot be denied, but that the fish is new in any way certainly can be.... There is no doubt that the sea trout and the brook trout are one and the same fish. It is broadly claimed that any of the trout can live as well in salt water as they can in fresh water, and everything seems to prove the claim to be correct. All trout grow to a larger size in salt water than in the brooks or rivers, and they 97 lose their spots in the sea, becoming pale and silvery in color. Brook trout were originally found at a distance not greater than three hundred miles back from the ocean in waters tributary to it. Where conditions of temperature were favorable, they invariably sought salt water. When transplanted to, or found in, inland waters, they have adapted themselves to fresh-water conditions as well. All members of the trout family require cold water for their habitat, averaging about 68 degrees or less. Therefore, they must either seek the cold water of the ocean, or, if barred from that by long stretches of warm-river waters, they must seek the cold, small tributaries high up in the hills. While trout are found in the highland streams south of New York as far as South Carolina, they are not able to seek the sea on account of the warm, intervening waters. In Long Island (N. Y.) streams all trout are sea-going. From that point along the coast northward sea trout are rarely, if ever, found until the northern shores of Maine and New Brunswick are reached. All rivers flowing into the St. Lawrence as far west as Quebec, as well as those entering the Saguenay and those of the Labrador coast, are especially noted for most excellent sea trout fishing, and are the favorite resorts of Anglers.... In all ways the sea trout corresponds with the brook trout when taken in fresh water. If taken in salt water, there will only be the variation of coloring. ... ouananiche ... and sea trout ... with the exception of salmon ... afford the greatest sport that the Angler can find.... Exactly the same tackle is used (for sea trout) as for ouananiche, trout, or bass, and the same flies, both in kind and size.... When the fish begin to leave the sea and ascend the 98 rivers, the bright colorings not only return, but actually appear to be more beautiful than those of the trout that always remain in fresh water.... But little attention, comparatively speaking, has been given to sea trout, principally because their nature was not understood, and, in fact, but little has been said or written in regard to them to arouse interest. The lessees of the sea trout streams on Long Island are very enthusiastic over the fishing they secure, as are those sportsmen who have sought it in Canada. The Canadian rivers are now more quickly and easily reached than formerly, and as the fish are rapidly acquiring fame they are bound to become much sought after by Anglers. However, sea trout fishing is but fishing for brook trout under different conditions, and amid varied surroundings. They offer, however, two extra inducements—they are more plentiful and usually average larger."

Charles Hallock (Sportsman's Gazetteer) refers to the common theory that sea trout (Canada) are merely a clan or detachment of the brook trout which have temporarily left their fresh-water haunts for the sea; then Mr. Hallock asks: "But, if we must accept this as a postulate, we must be permitted to ask why the same peculiarities do not attach to the trout of Maine. Cape Cod, and Long Island? Why do we not discover here this periodical midsummer advent and 'run' of six weeks' duration; and why are only isolated individuals taken in the salt-water pound nets and fykes of Long Island, etc., instead of thousands, as in Canada? Moreover, the Canadian sea trout are never taken in the small streams, but only in rivers of considerable size, and the same trout uniformly return to the same river, just as salmon do—at least, we infer so 99 from the fact that six-pounders are invariably found in the Nouvelle, and varying sizes elsewhere. Besides, we must be able to answer why a portion only of the trout in a given stream should periodically visit the sea at a specified time, while an equal or greater number elect to remain behind in fresh water; for we may suppose that, having equal opportunities, all have the same instincts and desires."

But, trout of different localities do not have equal opportunities; therefore, they have not the same instincts and desires. Local conditions of Nature everywhere guide the instincts and govern the desires of every living thing. So, the trout of Maine, the trout of Cape Cod, the trout of Long Island—influenced by local conditions—are all vastly different in opportunities, instincts, desires, etc. The Eskimo biped, the African biped—the bipeds of all countries—are all species of the animal man, but who dare suggest that they all have equal (similar) opportunities and the same instincts and desires?

Even individuals of the trout of one community are profoundly separated in character from their immediate brothers and sisters. Trout vary in their tastes and antics as they vary in color, shape, and size. There are hundreds of natural trout flies and hundreds of artificial trout flies, imitations of the living insects, used as lures in fishing. Why so many patterns? Because the trout, like man, is in love with a variety of foods at different times, and both man and trout change in their tastes by the month, the week, the day, the hour, and the minute.

The Angler does not have to use the hundreds of fly patterns at one fishing, but he does experiment with a variety of the lures to find the particular patterns 100 the fish is responsive to at the moment. One or two patterns would suffice—if the Angler could select the particular species the trout are rising to without trying all the patterns until he discovers the killing patterns. A chef might please his master with one or two of the forty courses billed if he knew what the man wanted. Sometimes the Angler can judge the appropriate fly to use by observing Nature in seeing trout rise to the live fly; but there are times when trout are not rising, times when they are tired of the fly upon the water, and times when the real fly is not on the wing.

General rules are of no service without a deep regard for general conditions, local and otherwise. All trout must not be judged alike even if they be of one species and in one little pool. Individuals of man, though of one race and in one district, are not all alike in their habits any more than they are in their shades, shapes, and sizes.

The conditions of the large rivers of Newfoundland are different from the conditions of the small streams of Maine, Long Island, and Cape Cod; hence the differing desires of the trout in these differing waters. There is no similarity in the quiet, tiny trout brooks of Long Island and the broad torrential rivers of Newfoundland, and it is only natural that the fishes of these deeply contrasting waters should be widely separated in character—instinct, desires, color, shape, size, etc. So I do not hesitate to express a belief that the sea trout, no matter where we find it, is just our own fond fontinalis incognito.

Between Halifax and Sydney, Nova Scotia, there are many wild sea trout rivers where the fish have never seen a human being. Angle from the middle of 101 June to the end of August. In June large sea trout are caught in salt water at the mouth of rivers on the artificial fly and minnow bait. The best east shore sea trout streams are St. Mary's, Muscadoboit. Tangier, Cole Harbor, Petpeswick, Quoddy, Sheet Harbor, Moser's River, Half-way Brook, Smith Brook, Ecwon Secum, Isaac's Harbor, and about Guysboro.

Southwest of Halifax great sea trout fishing may be had at Ingram River, Nine Mile River, Hubley's. Indian River, and about Liverpool, Chester, and the salmon country about Medway.

In New Brunswick beautiful and prolific sea trout waters may be reached from the towns of New Castle (Miramichi River and branches—May and June). Chatham (Miramichi River, Tabusintac River, Bartibog River, Eskeldoc River), Bathhurst (Nipisguit River, Tetagouche River, Caroquet River, Pockmouche River), and Campbellton, in the Baie de Chaleur River, Restigouche River, and the Cascapedia. Metapedia, Upsalquitch, Nouvelle, Escuminac rivers.

My choice of sea trout flies includes: Brown Hackle. Claret, Cinamon, Codun, Jenny Lind, Parmachenee Belle, Montreal, Grouse, Silver Doctor. Use sober-hued patterns in fresh water; bright patterns in salt water. Hooks: Nos. 7 to 12.

102

CHAPTER XVI

HOOKING THE TROUT

"Give plenty of time for the fish to swallow the hook," says O. W. Smith, in Outdoor Life (December, 1914), addressing the croppie (strawberry bass) Angler.

It is not un-anglerlike to catch any fish hooked beyond the lips? Angling has its gentle qualities as well as its practical ends. It's different in mere fishing. I don't believe any Angler would purposely hook his game otherwise than in the lip—a nerveless center where there is no pain—though the plain fisherman may resort to any method in his pursuit.

I remember some years ago when two fishermen caught the same fish (a large fluke), one hook being in the fish's mouth and the other hook on the inside of the fish's stomach, it was decided after a long discussion that the fish really belonged to the man whose hook held to the mouth; the swallowed hook was judged as illegitimate.

Fishes hooked in the mouth do not suffer any pain. I've recaught many a once-lost specimen with my snell in its lip; these in both fresh water and salt water. Incidents of this character furnish one of the many proofs that mouth-hooking the fish is perfectly humane. Two friends witnessed my catch (July 11, 1915) of a Long Island two-and-one-quarter-pound brook trout 103 that had a fly and leader (my first cast) dangling from its mouth, the gear he broke away with a few minutes before his actual capture.

There is no need of subjecting fishes to any pain in angling. Hook them in the lips, and kill them the very second they are taken from the water. Letting them die slowly not only pains the captured fishes, but injures them as food.

Be a sportsman in angling as well as in hunting. The chivalric gunner, unlike the market shooter, does not pot his quail huddled stationary on the ground; he gallantly takes it on the wing—gives it a fair chance. So the Angler, unlike the trade fisher, gives his game fair play. I catch quite my share of many species of fishes, but I only rarely suffer them to swallow the bait, and this by accident. Even pickerel and fluke (plaice) can be abundantly taken by being hooked in the lips. I never allow the pickerel or the black bass to swallow the bait; I hook them in the lip as I hook my trout—on the wing, as it were.

104

CHAPTER XVII

DOCTOR NATURE

"The wise for cure on exercise depend;
God never made His work for man to mend."

"He that takes no holiday hastens a long rest."
Game is not the only thing sought for by many men and women who go angling and shooting. Wise Lord Russell used to ride to the hounds until he bagged an appetite, then turn suddenly and ride as hard as possible to the nearest farmhouse and eat a hearty meal. Audubon and Wilson went afield to study ornithology; Gray and Thoreau for the study of general natural history, and thousands upon thousands of men and women less famous have gone afield with rod and gun for still another quarry—health.

Lord Russell's appetite hunting reminds me of the case of a young invalid whom I once took on a trout fishing trip. The young man had been ill all his life. Nobody seemed to know what his complaint was, but everybody he came in contact with agreed that he was ill. He looked it, and often said he was born that way. I defined his case the first day I met him—the city complaint, a complication of general under-the-weather-ness that is brought about by foul air, improper exercise, steady indoor work, irregularity, cigarettes, and incorrect food incorrectly eaten. He's well now. He went out in the woods for two weeks 105 every three months for six years, and at present he's as fat and solid as a Delaware shad. I shall never forget his expression when he hooked his first breath of fresh air and creeled a genuine outdoor appetite. A woods appetite is very different from the hunger that once in a while comes to the always-in-the-city man. It strikes suddenly, one's knees begin to shake, and a cold perspiration breaks out on the forehead. My poor young friend, having never previously experienced an appetite, of course didn't know what had taken hold of him. He began to cry and totter, and I stepped up to him just in time to save him from falling off a moss-covered rock into a roaring trout stream.

"I'm ill," he said, "have been ill all my life. I thought this trip would do me good but I'm worse. Please let me lie down; I'm very faint."

"Oh, come," said I, "you're only hungry; here, give me your rod, and lean on my arm; you'll be all right in a little while."

I took him up to the farmhouse and started him slowly on some deviled trout and watercress. Poor fellow, he reminded me of a young setter dog born and brought up in the city and taken afield for the first time. Well, that young man did nothing but cry and eat for two weeks. He then went home to tell his folks he had come to life, and then hurried out to feed and weep for another month. I know a hundred young men and women in New York who are in a bad way with the city complaint. The streets are filled with ghost-like creatures. Lord Derby is right: "If you do not find time for exercise you will have to find time for illness."

"To-morrow we will go a-fishing; do thou go now and fetch the bait."—Hymir to Thar.

106

CHAPTER XVIII

THE BROOK TROUT

"Then, give me the trout of the mountain stream.
With his crimson stars and his golden gleam;
When he, like a hero, on the moss lies.
The Angler has won his fairest prize!"
Author Unknown.

Trout Taking Flies.—"Trout invariably strike the insect first with their tails, knocking it into the water and then devouring it with a swift dart which can hardly be distinguished from the original movement, so quickly does one succeed the other."—W. C. Prime.

Trout Colors.—The color of a trout's back depends on the color of the bottom of the river. Rapidly growing trout differ greatly in spots and color from those which grow slowly and thrive badly. A middle-aged trout differs in color from an aged trout. Speaking generally, the young, healthy, fast-growing fish will have silvery sides, white belly, and plenty of well-defined spots. The poorly fed fish will have few or no spots, a drab belly, and muddy yellow sides. Old trout are particularly lank and large-headed.

Tame Trout.—An English gentleman has two brook trout that take flies from his fingers, and that ring a 107 little bell cord when they are hungry. They were taught this latter performance by having bits of food tied to the cord when it was first introduced.

Wild Trout and Tame.—"Somehow the catching of, as it were, stall-fed trout has not the same charm as the fishing for the wild trout. The domestics lack that fierce rush and dash of the wild beauty."—John B. Robinson.

Sight, Hearing, etc., of Trout.—"There is no question ... as to the high development of the senses of sight, taste, and hearing in trout."—Wm. C. Harris.

Trout at Play.—"Many times have I leaned over the sides of my boat in Northern waters, where the trout lay beneath me, and seen the mottled beauties chase each other, and race and leap in rivalry of sport, until their bright sides irradiated the dark stream with glancing light, as if the rays of the sun had taken water and were at their bath."—W. H. H. Murry.

Trout in Hungary.—The streams of Hungary afford excellent angling for trout and grayling.

Unidentified Trout.—M. P. Dunham of Ovando. Montana, a sportsman's guide of many years' experience, writes me: "We have two trout here in Montana that I do not find pictured in The Angler's Guide or any other book I have seen containing the technical portraits of the fishes. One of these trout weighs up to forty-nine pounds and its average weights are twelve pounds to fifteen pounds. The other is a small trout that averages less than one pound in weight, and it 108 has no spots. The large trout has a few spots, these being particularly brilliant in the mating season—September and October. The best time to fish for this large species is in August and September. Both of these unidentified trout will rise to the artificial fly, but in fly-fishing I have never taken a specimen of the large species that weighed over six pounds, the fish ranging beyond this weight favoring small fish and red meat for bait. The waters are overstocked with the large variety; the small unspotted variety is only in one stream." Undoubtedly these two trout are odd forms of well-known species. Mr. Dunham should send specimens of each to the United States Fish Commission at Washington. The small trout will undoubtedly prove to be the common mountain trout, whose peculiar habitat—the one stream Mr. Dunham mentions—is responsible for its peculiar coloring. The large fish that ranges up to forty-nine pounds is no doubt a form of lake trout which has been known to attain a weight of eighty pounds and a length of six feet.

The Trout's Symmetry.—"Few humanly designed lines are more graceful than those of the yacht. The trout is made up of such lines. It is a submarine designed by the Almighty. It makes the most of the simple elements of artistic beauty—symmetry of line, suggestive of agile power, and delicately blended harmonies of rich color."—New York Evening Telegram, editorial page, July 17, 1915.

The Beautiful Trout.—"Of all the many species of trout, Salvelinus or Salmo, the brook trout, fontinalis, is by far the most beautiful."—Charles Zibeon Southard.

109

A Loving Trout.—At the Wintergreen estate, Highland Lake, Winsted, Conn., a brook trout was kept in captivity in a deep spring for seven years. When the fish was fifteen inches in length two other brook trout, a male and female, each ten inches long, were placed in the spring to keep the old fellow company. He promptly fell in love with the lady trout and killed and swallowed her escort.

Albino Trout.—The fish hatchery in St. Paul, Minn., had at one time twenty thousand albino trout in stock. This species was discovered in 1893. There is something peculiar in Minnesota waters which aids propagation of this species. The fish are white mottled with red and yellow spots; the fins are white with red bands mottled with yellow. The eyes are red and the trout has apparently a transparent skin so that the bones are visible through it.

Rainbow Trout.—Dr. A. E. Buzard, of Hayward. Calif., fishing in the Spokane River within ten minutes' walk of the city of Spokane, Wash., creeled eleven rainbow trout weighing, collectively, seventeen pounds.

Rocky Mountain Trout.—H. E. Peck, of Kenman. North Dakota, and H. N. Stabeck, of Minneapolis. Minn., enjoyed good trout fishing last summer in the Crow West country of the Rocky Mountains. A catch of thirty-one trout weighed, collectively, fifty-one pounds. The largest specimen weighed three and one fourth pounds.

Flood-water Trout.—When the trout stream is flooded, the trout find plenty of food and they gorge 110 themselves with worms, etc. Then they refuse the Angler's bait for several days—"trout feed on a rising stream, not on a falling stream."—E. Curley.

A Tame Trout.—"Sunbeam, the pet speckled trout in the fish hatchery at Estes Park, is very fond of being stroked and petted, and will swim around and rub itself against a person's hand whenever a chance is given it."—Estes (Calif.) Correspondent New York World. I'll warrant this fish only rubs its lips against the hand of man. No fish will willingly allow its body to come in contact with a man's hand, because fishes are covered with a slime that protects them when they encounter rocks, logs, etc., and they naturally would not voluntarily waste this valuable armor.

Traits of the Trout.—The brook trout (Salvelinus fontinalis), using its tail with vigor and precision, will splash water into the midst of a mass of flying insects (midge, black gnat, mosquito, etc.), and thus disable these insects so that they will fall on the surface of the water, where they become easy prey to the voracious trout. Fontinalis will also use his tail in striking to disable larger insects (butterflies, beetles, cricket, potato-bug, etc.), and the Angler's artificial flies when they are floating in or upon the water.

Rainbow Trout.—"The rainbow takes the fly so readily that there is no reason for resorting to grasshoppers, salmon eggs, or other bait. It is a fish whose gameness will satisfy the most exacting of expert Anglers, and whose readiness to take any proper line will please the most impatient of inexperienced amateurs."—Prof. Evermann.

111

The Tactful Trout.—"Trout are emblems of quiet, calm, and gentleness, such as love not to be in troubled waters or to be tossed to and fro by the blustering of wicked and malevolent spirits, but rather live quiet at home than enjoy abundance through labor and trouble."—Randal Holme.

Double-headed Trout.—A two-headed brook trout is the product of the fish hatchery at Colebrook, N. H.

Trout in Side Currents.—"As a general rule although many trout are taken near, very near the rough, white water of a stream, they do not as a rule lie in the very swiftest portions, but in adjacent and quieter side currents."—Samuel G. Camp.

The Angler's Joy.—"The brook trout always will be the Angler's greatest joy, but the German brown trout [introduced in American waters and the rainbow trout add variety to the social life of the streams."—Neal Brown.

112

CHAPTER XIX

THE ANGLER

"I live not in myself, but I become
Portion of that around me; and to me
High mountains are a feeling, but the hum
Of human cities torture."
Byron.
"He'd eat his lunch in a minute;
He had no time to spare.
At a mounted fish in a window
He'd stop an hour to stare."
Judge.

The Lone Angler.—"The reason a man likes to go angling is that his family doesn't like to go with him."—New York Press.

The True Angler.—"If true Anglers, you are sure to be gentle; and as the truly gentle are always virtuous, you must be happy. Let neither prosperity nor adversity deaden 'the fresh feeling after Nature' which the use of the rod and reel always heightens or confers. Whether overladen with good fortune or suffering under the shocks of adversity, forget not to take the magic wand and repair to the murmuring waters. 'The music of those gentle moralists will steal into your heart'; and, while invigorating physical energy, your souls will be charmed and your minds 113 soothed and tempered by the melody of birds, the sights of nature, and the sounds of inferior animals above, around, and beneath the enlivening waters. With rosy dreams and bright streams, breezy morns and mellow skies, a light heart and a clear conscience, may 'God speed ye well.'"—Genio C. Scott, Fishing in American Waters.

Real vs. Rural Angler.—The assertion that the bent-pin-fishing country boy can catch more trout than the properly equipped Angler is material of the comic papers. No impracticable boy, whether he be of the country or of the city, can excel the correctly rigged, careful Angler. The bent-pin youth of the farm may outfish the unskillful, showy tyro from the city, but to compete with the scientific Angler he would have about the same chance of outfishing the expert as a cow would have fishing alongside of a mink.

The Bicycle Angler.—Mr. David Rivers writes me: "I ride my wheel to my favorite angling places regularly in the spring, summer, and autumn times. The four-ounce rod takes up no noticeable space on the wheel, and my leader-box and fly-book are easily carried in my pockets."

The Determined Angler.—"There is peculiar pleasure in catching a trout in a place where nobody thinks of looking for them, and at an hour when everybody believes they cannot be caught."—Henry van Dyke.

Dry and Wet Fly Angler.—"Startling as the statement may sound, it is probably true that the really 114 good wet-fly fisherman is a greater rarity than the really good dry-fly man."—London Field.

The Expert Fly Angler.—"A real expert with the wet-fly is a much rarer bird than one with the dry."—London Fishing Gazette.

The Finished Fly Angler.—= " ... to be a finished wet-fly Angler one must possess as much skill as the dry-fly fisherman."—Emlyn M. Gill.

The Angler Body and Soul.—"To take fish is only the body of the gentle art. Some of its real enjoyments are what the Angler sees and feels—the echo of the running streams, the music of the birds, the beauty of the flowers peering at him from every side, the bracing atmosphere, the odor of pines, hemlocks, and spruce; the hush of the woods at night, the morning song of the robin, and the revived appetite."—A. L. H.

Ye Gude Angler.—"Wha ever heard o' a gude angler being a bad or indifferent man?"—Noctes.

The Merry Angler.—"And if the angler take fysshe: surely thenne is there noo man merier than he is in his spyryte."—Dame Juliana Berners (1496).

The Religious Angler.—"The old man fished not for pastime, nor solely for a subsistence, but as a solemn sacrament and withdrawal from the world, just as the aged read their Bible."—Thoreau.

The Satisfied Angler.—Trout in the creel or no trout in the creel, the Angler never complains of poor 115 sport if there be trout in the water he fishes, if the weather be pleasant, and the scenery fair. Some fishermen judge their day by the actual catch of fish. The true rodster loves the pursuit and capture of the fish, the bright day, and the beautiful natural surroundings equally well.

The Tidy Angler.—I don't care if the fish I catch weigh only a pound, no matter what the species may be. My tackle is light, fine, and properly rigged, and with it, in taking big fish or half-pound and pound fish, I have just as much sport as the man who uses heavy, coarse, ill-kept tackle on bigger game alone. The woodcock—the king of game birds—is bagged with No. 10 shot, but the sport of taking it is quite as great as the shooting of fowl ten times its size.

The Assiduous Angler.—The constant-in-application man becomes the practical fisherman.

The Compleat Angler.—"Walton's book is as fresh as a handful of wild violets and sweet lavender. It breathes the odors of green fields and woods."—Henry van Dyke.

The Literary Angler.—Izaak Walton's famous work, The Compleat Angler, or the Contemplative Man's Recreation, a copy of the first edition, small 8vo, original sheep binding, London, 1653, brought the highest price of the day (April 9, 1915) at the sale of the library of the late General Brayton Ives at the American Art Galleries, New York, $2475. George D. Smith was the successful bidder. The record price for this edition is $6000, which was paid at the sale of 116 the library of W. C. Van Antwerp of New York some years ago at Sotheby's in London by the late Bernard Quaritch, acting as agent for the late J. Pierpont Morgan, in whose collection the valuable volume now is.

A Centenarian Angler.—Mrs. Jane T. Rinkle of Bristol, Tenn., is over one hundred years of age. Still vigorous for one of her years, Mrs. Rinkle believes that her long life and her bright prospect for living some years longer is due to her fondness for angling. "I have hardly passed a fishing season in fifty years," said the old lady at her last anniversary party, "that I have not gone to the river with hook and line."

The Woman Angler.—The Duchess of Bedford has the distinction of a record catch of English salmon. Her creel for one day numbered thirteen, the greatest string of salmon ever taken in a single day by a woman. Three other prominent English women Anglers are Lady Sybil Grey, daughter of Earl Grey, Milicent. Duchess of Sutherland, and Lady Rosemary Portal, only child of the second Earl of Cairns. Each of these ladies are highly expert in fly-casting.

The Waltonian Angler.—"It matters not at all what trout waters the Angler fishes if he has the true and kindly spirit of Izaak Walton, the Master Angler of years ago; for then every stream and lake has its own peculiar and delightful charms in which the Angler revels while angling, with either the wet or the dry fly, to fathom their piscatorial secrets. Of all sport. I know of none that seems to develop in the individual such a kindly spirit, such a full appreciation of all 117 living things, and such an absorbing love for the many and varied charms of 'the open' as fly-fishing."—Charles Zibeon Southard.

The Merciful Angler.—The names of three members of a recent jury in the County Court of Brooklyn. N. Y., were Fish, Fisher, and Fishline—a trio of honest men, no doubt. With Bates and Waters added, this jury would have little trouble in mercifully holding up the scales of justice.

The Peaceful Angler.—"Don't think of your business or profession while fishing. Forget your desk, your pen, and also your debts and your enemies, if you have any."—"The Professor."

The Mathematical Angler.—"His rule in fishing was to fish in the difficult places which others were likely to skip."—Daniel Webster.

The Ever-Youthful Angler.—"Don't become old—go fishing once or twice a week."—"The Professor."

The Halcyonian Angler.—"The whole arcana book of trout fishing consists in rather the mental construction of the Angler than in the manner and method of the process. The fish is a convenient peg, so to say, on which we hang the dolce far niente, and render the day's sport in its pursuit halcyon and superlative. The sport itself may be insufficient, but there is always some recompense in the effort made and in the close communion with 'dear nature's self.' Not always do large bags and great results crown the Angler's desire. Too often it is far otherwise, and yet the true Angler 118 never feels like giving up fishing because of poor sport."—John Harrington Keene.

The Luxuriant Angler.—James L. Breeze's string of salmon pools in Restigouche cost this enthusiastic Angler $35,000.

The Concentrated Angler.—"A gentleman hesitates to bother anybody whose mind is concentrated on his fishing. The expert knows by experience one question leads to another, then on to begging, borrowing, or buying. The expert knows that tyros are never provided with tackle, bait, or reasonable consideration for others. They expect the whole boatload of Anglers to wait on them because they catch no fish."—Louis Rhead.

The Home Angler.—"The sporting element among fishermen haven't any fine sensibilities ... the true fishermen fish for edible fish only for their own use and the use of their families."—"Piscator."

The Lost Angler.—"Remember that water always is supposed to run south, save in a few instances where it runs direct north or west from the mountains, as the Red River in Minnesota, flowing north, for instance. This certainly would be a misleader. But as a rule water runs south. Follow it. Along streams man makes his abode."—Robert Page Lincoln.

CHAPTER XX

ANGLING

"... which, as in no other game
A man may fish and praise His name."
W. Basse.
"I chose of foure good dysportes and honeste gamys, that is to wyte: of huntynge: hawkynge: fysshynge: and foulynge. The best to my symple dyscrecon why then is fysshynge: called Anglynge with a rodde: and a line and an hoke."—Dame Juliana Berners, The Treatyse of Fysshynge wyth an Angle, 1496.

"If the bending rod and the ringing reel
Give proof that you've fastened the tempered steel.
Be sure that the battle is but begun
And not till he's landed is victory won."
Author Unknown.
Fair and Foul Angling.—Anybody can catch a trout with a worm. This is the bait of the boy and the boatman. The Angler gives the trout a fair battle with the artificial fly. Comparing live-bait fishing to artificial fly angling is like comparing blacksmithry to jewel working, bronco breaking to genteel horsemanship, or buccaneering to yachting.

Refinement of Angling.—Angling is fishing governed by rules of chivalry—correct tackle, limit in the catch, and humane treatment of the game.

120

Landing the Fish.—"The surest way to take the fish is give her leave to play and yield her line."—Quarles, Shepheard's Eclogues, 1644. Subdue a big fish before you try to land him. Don't be in a hurry. Give him line, but keep it taut (not tight), and don't become excited. Don't try to yank him out of his element or pull him through the line guides. Raise the rod tip over the back of your head, and don't grab the line—guide the game into the landing net or up to the gaff. Take your time. Be glad if the fish escapes. His life is as important as yours—to him, at least. Besides, you'd soon tire of fishing if you never lost a fish. "The play's the thing" in angling, anyway, because, as an Angler, you can buy fish cheaper than you can catch them, if you play fair—if you're not of the gentry that judge the day by quantity instead of quality. Some of the greatest Anglers are the poorest fish killers, but to them one fish correctly captured on chivalric tackle means more than a tubful of butchered victims means to the unenlightened bungler. Contrast and conditions count for something in everything. If there were no cloudy days we'd never correctly value the sunshine. Method in the pursuit, appropriateness of the equipment, and uncertainty in the catch, wholly distasteful to the selfish neophyte, are thoroughly appreciated by the Angler.

Ancient Angling.—One of the most ancient literary works on fishing, perhaps the most ancient of all really known volumes on the subject, is Hauleutics of Oppian, the work of a Greek poet, A.D. 198, from which many articles on fishing and angling, thought to be modern, have been taken. Athenæus tells us 121 that several writers wrote treatises or poems on fishing centuries before the Christian era.

Old Angling Books.—1486—The Booke of St. Albans; by Dame Juliana Berners. 1590—Booke of Fishing with Hook and Line; by Leonard Mascall. 1596—Hawking. Hunting, Fowling and Fishing; by W. C. Faukener. 1606—Booke of Angling or Fishing; by Samuel Gardner, D.D. 1651—Art of Angling; by Thomas Barker (the second edition of this book, published in 1657, was issued under the title of Barker's Delight). 1652—Young Sportsman's Delight and Instructor in Angling, etc.; by Gervase Markham. 1653—The Compleat Angler, or the Contemplative Man's Recreation, etc.; by Izaak Walton (the second edition, almost rewritten by the author, appeared in 1655). 1662—Experienced Angler, or Angling Improved; by Robert Venables. 1676—Angler's Delight, etc.; by William Gilbert. 1681—Angler's Vade Mecum; by Chetham. 1682—Complete Troller; by Nobles. 1696—The True Art of Angling; by J. S.

Carrying the Rod.—Joint your rod only when you reach the place of angling, and take it apart again when you are ready to leave the water for camp, unless the camp is on the edge of the lake or stream. When angling along thickly wooded banks, carry the rod in front of you, tip first, pointing the tip through the bushes you penetrate; never pull it after you. Fasten the hook on one of the reel bars, and then thrust the rod's tip through the branches or shrubbery ahead of you when you move along, casting here and there. This is not necessary when one only moves a step or two, for then, if there be open space, the rod 122 and line may be held clear of the underbrush and branches. In all cases keep the rod ahead of you. When disjointed, the rod pieces may be held together by small rubber bands until the rod case is made use of, but don't lay the rod away with the rubber bands intact, as the rubber will bend the tip out of shape, dislodge the wood coating, disturb the whipping, and tarnish the ferrules. Dr. E. F. Conyngham of Bonner. Mont., doesn't like my notion of carrying the rod tip first. The Doctor says he favors carrying it butt first with the tip trailing behind. "I have fished with a fly for trout and salmon nearly forty years in Europe and this continent," says the Doctor, "and never yet saw an expert Angler carry a rod in the way described by Mr. Bradford. That is just the proper caper to break tips. The rod in going through brush should be carried butt forward; then the tip will trail as easily as the tail on a dog, and furthermore, you can walk at good speed without interference. In my many years of fly fishing I have had one broken tip; a woman knocked it down and stepped on it. Luckily it was lancewood, so I could repair it. What would have been my predicament had the rod been of split bamboo?" Very good, Doctor. I may be wrong but, I learned my way from my fathers of the angle—Seth Green. John Harrington Keene, Frederick Mather, William C. Harris, et al.—when I was being taught first lessons in fly-fishing. Seth Green, John Keene, and Harris personally advised me to carry the fly rod tip in front of me, and each of the trio personally showed me the method on the trout streams. Harris and Keene always carried their fly rods tip first, and I have seen both these experts along the streams many times during many years of personal fishing with both of 123 these Anglers. However, Dr. Conyngham must not be denied his view on the subject. Just as there are famous wing shots who shoot with one eye closed and other experts who give trigger with both eyes open, so in angling, there are many practiced hands who disagree on the various ways and means in fishing. I favor keeping my tip in front of me, and while I shall never change this method, I refrain from condemning Dr. Conyngham's contrastive way of carrying his tip. Charles Zibeon Southard agrees with both the Doctor and me. He advises carrying the tip ahead in the open and behind in the brush.

The Angling World.—"Angling takes us from the confusion, the filth, and the social and moral degradation of the big cities and places us in close contact with one of the most important divisions of human labor—the cultivation of the soil, which is the real foundation of all national wealth and true social happiness. Everything connected with the land is calculated to foster the best and noblest feelings of the soul and to give the mind the most lofty and sublime ideas of universal nature. To men of contemplative habits the roaming along brooks, rivers, lakes, and fields gives rise to the most refined intellectual enjoyment. Such persons move in a world of their own and experience joys and sorrows with which the world cannot meddle."—A. L. H.

Colorado Trout Streams.—Colorado has six thousand miles of trout streams.

Angling Saves Words.—"Contemplation and quietness! Will these words soon be labeled in our dictionaries 124 'obsolete'? It would seem so; yet there will be some use for them, among old-fashioned folk, as long as the word 'angling' holds its place."—Willis Boyd Allen.

Large-Trout Angling.—Frank Brigg, of London. England, fishing in New River, caught an eighteen-pound trout, the heaviest specimen of trout ever taken in a London water.

Speculation in Angling.—"I often wonder if the basis of fishing is not founded upon the element of chance, and whether fishing does not fascinate because it is a species of gambling. To a degree it is a hazard. You take your best tackle, select your choicest bait, and you do more, for you pray to the goddess of success."—"Ancient Mariner."

Economy in Angling.—"Don't take more fish than you can use; if you do, you take that which belongs to someone else."—"Tops'l."

An Angling Classic.—"Angling is the only sport that boasts the honor of having given a classic [Izaak Walton's The Compleat Angler, 1653 to literature."—Henry van Dyke.

How to Approach a Trout.—" ... sense of hearing in all species of fish is a matter of concussion on the surface of the water. Sit motionless in a boat, and you may sing, "I Won't Go Home 'Til Morning," or any other gala song, to the extreme high limit of your voices, and the trout or any other fish will remain undisturbed, but, scratch your toe upon the bottom of 125 the boat, and presto! the pool is as dead and barren as a burned prairie. Approach a pool from over the bank with a careless tread, and when you reach it the trout are gone, none know where. Crawl to the pool noiselessly on all fours and you will find your trout reposing without fear of danger. The avoidance of concussion is the great factor on a trout pool or stream in getting a satisfactory creel. Slide, rather than step, in wading, and your success will be greater."—Wm. C. Harris.

Strike from the Reel or Hand?—"The strike must be made with sufficient force and no more. If insufficient, the hook will not penetrate far enough to hold the fish in its subsequent struggles, and if the force is excessive the gut will break at its weakest point, and leave the fly and possibly one or more strands of gut in the trout's jaws. The Angler should acquire the habit of striking from the reel, i.e., without holding the line in the hand. Many old fishermen prefer holding the line when striking, but it is at best a risky proceeding, and too likely to result in a breakage of the gut."—F. M. Halford, The Dry-Fly Man's Handbook. "Personally I never 'strike from the reel' ... because less control is had over the line, likewise the fish."—Charles Zibeon Southard, Trout Fly-Fishing in America. I favor Mr. Halford's method—"strike from the reel"—in fly-fishing and in weakfish fishing with light tackle. In heavy bait fishing, Mr. Southard's strike with the "hand-held line" suits me.

The Silver Hook.—"There is a good deal of fun in thinking you are going to have it."—New York Press.

126 True; Walton says the Angler's anticipation of fishing is as great a joy as the realization of it.

Angling Ailment.—"We never get over the fishing fever; it is a delightful disease, and, thank the Lord, there is no cure."—Ira W. Moore.

Angling and Nature.—"Association with men of the world narrows the heart; communion with nature expands it."—Jean Paul Richter.

Angling and Mathematics.—"Angling may be said to be so much like the Mathematics, that it can ne'er be fully learnt; at least not so fully, but that there will still be more new experiments left for the tryal of other men that succeed us."—Izaak Walton, The Compleat Angler, 1653.

Tendency of Angling.—"I am now over 76 [years in age and owe my life to fishing, and I find the tendency of fishing is to make one careful, artful, patient, and practical."—"Watcher."

Angling a Science.—"Angling is a science, not merely a pastime. It will broaden you and start your boy in a manly sport that will draw him to the country instead of to the dance hall, to the fields and streams instead of to the pool room."—"Greenhorn."

Fly vs. Worm.—"That fly-fishing is clean, and free from the muscular efforts of mountain-climbing; that it is usually rewarded with larger fish than those taken with a worm; that it has a freedom, a jollity, a certain broad, wide-spaced exhilaration, I willingly admit. 127 But, the humbler, old-fashioned method has a charm of its own which I am not ready to forego."—Willis Boyd Allen.

"Ye Gods and Little Fishes."—"When we have become familiar with the great cities with their bewildering sights and distracting sounds, the finest things remain to be discovered, and these discoveries must be made as we stand open-eyed in the presence of God's workmanship. Hills and streams, woods and flowers, bees and birds and butterflies, the flora and fauna of this earth where we have our home for a little time, should, somehow, be brought into the life of the child. The boy who grows up into manhood without being privileged to know the world of nature by personal contact has been robbed. He may be intelligent in many things and a useful member of society, but he has missed out of life some of its deepest satisfactions and purest joys. Indeed, such an one is not symmetrically educated, and is quite likely to be put to shame as the years pass by."—Lathan A. Crandall, Days in the Open.

Angling Is its Own Reward.—"No other sportsman brings home more from his sport than he takes to it than the fisherman. His basket is heavy with present food in the morning, and loaded with future food in the afternoon, with an appetite and a sleepetite that requires three days to satisfy."—Hy. Julius.

Ideal Angling Time.—The last two weeks in June—what lovelier period for brook trout fishing in the rich flower-lined mountain streams? When does the wild shrub smell sweeter than now, the wind blow more 128 balmily, the songbirds trill sweeter, and the spotted trout bite better?

Landing the Trout.—The proper time to spend in landing a fish all depends upon the condition of your fishing ground. Lead your prize away from obstructions, keep the line taut, and do not nervously hurry the play. Take your time.

Fishes' Feeding-Time.—Fishes are said to bite better between the new moon and the first quarter; or between the last quarter and the change.

Calmness in Angling.—Don't hurry a large fish. Subdue him as far from you as possible.

Shadowless Angling.—Never let your shadow fall upon the angling water. Keep the sun in front of you.

Striking and Hooking.—Nothing is more difficult to learn about fly-fishing than the art of striking or hooking the game.

The Fishless Fisherman.—"You took a day off from your work and went fishing? Have any luck?" "Certainly. A day off is luck enough."—New York American.

Angling Spirit.—"It is the way we do things and the spirit in which we prosecute our endeavors that counts. The man who takes the day to go fishing on the great ocean or in the forest and can commune with Nature can be as good a Christian as the best man that 129 ever entered the portals of a church, cathedral, or synagogue."—"Nature Factor."

All Sports in Angling.—"The sport that sums up dancing, song and picture, athletics and all games of chance is angling. The waves make you dance, all pictures roll before you, any chance can win the pool, and every fishing boat is a sängerfest. "—B. M. Briggs.

Early Trout Angling.—"Don't let anyone tell you of the folly of trout fishing in early April. It's great sport, and if you're skillful enough to get a few of the gamest and wisest fish that swims at this time of the year your success will be complete in May and June, when the ideal weather comes."—H. T. Walden.

Skill vs. Kill.—"To qualify as a sportsman in the taking of any kind of game, a man must show much more enthusiasm in skill rather than in the kill, always remembering to give or inflict the least pain possible on the game taken by his skill."—Wes' Wood.

Rainbow Trout Angling.—"I get harder play with a three-pound rainbow trout than with a maskinonge of twenty-five pounds. I have caught only a few rainbow trout. The first one I ever caught was three years ago in the Esopus Creek in the Catskills. I felt somewhat relieved when I had him in the net. He was the gamest fish for his size I ever hooked, and I have killed ten and twelve pound salmon on a trout rod. The rainbow trout is first cousin to the lordly salmon."—M. J. Doyle.

130

Secret of Angling.—"Fishing is more than catching. Its pleasures are the whole outdoors. Appreciation is the secret of the lure."—Theodore Macklin.

Limit in Angling.—"It is very foolish for Anglers, when they get more fishes than they want, to even give them away; far better it would be for them to stop fishing when they have caught enough for themselves, and give the fish a chance."—George Hartley.

Age of Angling.—"The allurement of fishing is as old as the granite mountains of the Andes. Down through the ages of the past, even from the day of the anthropophagi, comes to us the fact that all the world rejoices in the gentle art of fishing. Fishing—the one word that opens up to our understanding the philosophy of nature—is the fundamental basis of our civilization."—David Jones.

Gentility in Angling.—"Sportsmanship abhors greed and all vulgarity."—H. W. Wack.

Angling Clears the Brain.—"When we are confused and harried by the turmoil of modern life, our heads and our hearts aching with its complex problems, its exigent demands, its rebuffs, and its bitter disappointments, let us turn once more to the forest and meadow, the peaceful stream, with the fleecy clouds or overhanging boughs kindly tempering the rays of the summer sun; let us drop our pens, abandon for the nonce our manuscript, our ledgers, or the stock reports of the day, and 'go a-fishing.'"—Willis Boyd Allen.

131

Up and Down Stream.—"I fish up stream (and I think this best) and down stream and across stream—according to wind and time and weather, etc., and the sun. I have found I can get the larger fish in upstream fishing; but there are pools one can't get the flies to—the likely places—from below, nor yet from either side. When I come to such a pool I get above and cover it well by casting across stream from me—the sun being opposite—and let my flies float down, drawing them the while across current with a twitching motion, as an insect struggling to swim across. It is a deadly method if well done and gets the big ones too. I hold the line of course in my left hand, and as I gently raise the rod with my right, I take in line with my left, thus at all times having full control and ready for a strike."—Ernest L. Eubank.

Fly-Fishing First.—"Fly-fishing comes first, then comes bait casting with the fly rod; third, still fishing; fourth, casting of live bait with the short rod from the reel, and last, if not entirely without the pale of true sportsmanship, the use of the plug."—Rayx.

Fly Rod and Bait Rod.—"It takes some skill to keep sixty feet of line in the air when fly casting, and requires free space for the back cast. It is fascinating work and requires more delicacy in handling a fly rod than a bait rod. The fly rod, especially in Southern Missouri waters, lands more fish during the day than the bait rod, but the latter lands larger fish. The bait caster makes fewer casts on account of reeling in the line after each cast, but the water is more effectively covered. One has to be a judge of the water and determine which method should be used. In the 132 northern lakes bait casting is far superior in results to fly casting."—M. J. Brennan.

Land and Water.—"You're natural when fishing, and unnatural on shore. Fishing rubs the barnacles off your natural self, and makes your bodyship sail more easily."—B. M. Briggs.

First Record of Angling.—"The first authentic record of angling appears in the Old Testament of the Bible, computed to be about 1500 years before Christ, where the Lord asked Job: 'Canst thou take out a fish with the hook?'"—John Ryan.

Roman Angling.—The walls of Pompeii are adorned with angling scenes.

133

CHAPTER XXI

TROUT FLIES

"To make several flies
For the several skies.
That shall kill in despite of all weathers."
Charles Cotton.
Weight of Flies.—"Flies do not soon get tired; ... they are light; the wind carries them. An ounce of flies was once weighed, and afterwards counted; and it was found to comprise no less than six thousand two hundred and sixty-eight."—Victor Hugo, The Toilers of the Sea.

The Dry-Fly.—"Upon the curling surface let it glide, with natural motion from thy hand supplied."—Unknown Author. The italics in the word surface are ours. The dry artificial fly must swim on the surface, must fly upstream, must have no companion fly, must keep dry by sailing in the air between actual casts, and must attract the fish by minutely mimicking the living fly both in the air and on (not in) the water.

Vegetable Flies.—Bearded seed of the wild oat and a silvery willow leaf have been used successfully as artificial flies for brook trout and black bass.

134

To Carry Flies.—Do not use your large fly-book when wading. Put a half dozen seasonable patterns in your hatband, and a dozen more in a little book that will not bulge your pocket.

Variety in Flies.—You can never carry too many trout flies on your trip. Fill your fly-book and stick them all over the crown of your hat. Trout do not like the same fly at all times any more than you are fond of feeding on one sort of meat.

Clumsy Flies.—Most trout flies are too large, and they frighten more trout than they attract.

A New Fly.—" ... an altogether original fly, unheard of, startling, will often do great execution in an overfished pool."—Henry van Dyke.

The Floating Fly.—"The floating fly seemed to have the effect of arousing the trout to action at once. During the week I estimate that there was an average of ten rises to the dry-fly to every one to the same fly wet."—Emlyn M. Gill.

Fishing the Dry-Fly.—"The dry-fly is clearly out of place on the wet-fly water as the wet-fly is on the dry-fly stream. After all, it is only in the style of deceiving and hooking fish that dry-fly and wet-fly Anglers ... assuming both to be good sportsmen ... can much differ. In nearly all other fly-fishing matters they must naturally be at one. It has already been said that the dry-fly is quite out of place in many trout streams. The dry-fly streams, though they have increased of late years, are still and ever must be in 135 a decided minority. The dry-fly Angler is not, as a rule, a very early riser. He can do nothing without natural flies, and in my experience there are very few duns or other water-flies out till nine or even ten o'clock in the morning."—A. B. Dewar, The Book of the Dry-Fly.

American Dry-Flies.—"Whirling Dun, Wickham's Fancy, Pale Evening Dun, Jenny Spinner, (Hackle Fly), Willow Fly (Hackle Fly), Orange Fish Hawk (Hackle Fly), Olive Dun, Soldier Palmer (Hackle Fly). Silver Sedge, Red Spinner, White Miller, Coachman. Black Gnat."—Emlyn M. Gill, Practical Dry-Fly Fishing.

Brazilian Flies.—Brazilian flies, costing seven dollars a ton, are used to feed fishes in England.

Fresh Flies.—"When trout are taking the fly on the surface, and are not simply feeding on the larvæ as they swim upward, a brand new fly is more likely to catch a fish than one which has been a great deal used. I always use May-flies dressed on eyed hooks, have a goodly supply, and when one gets so wet as to necessitate a considerable amount of labor in the drying of it, off it comes, and is stuck in my cap to dry at its leisure. Of course it is rather wasting to the cast—this frequent changing flies—and no little trouble to those whose fingers are all thumbs, and whose eyesight is becoming dim, but it is far less trouble to change the fly than to dry it when thoroughly soaked."—London Fishing Gazette.

Rocky Mountain Trout Flies.—First, Royal Coachman; second, Gray Hackle with yellow body. Then: 136 Black Gnat, Ginger Quill, Cowdung, Blue Quill. Grizzly King, Shad Fly, and Stone Fly. Hooks, No. 6 to 14.

Early Season Flies.—Dark Stone, Codun, Alder. Bowman, Black May, Beauty, Ben Bent, Blue Bottle. Hare's Ear.

All-Season Flies.—Alder, Gray Palmer, Green Palmer, Ginger Palmer, March Brown, Reuben Wood. Professor, White Miller, Coachman, Royal Coachman. Dark Coachman, Codun, Scarlet Ibis, Brown Palmer. Red Palmer, Grizzly King, Queen of the Water, King of the Water, Brown Hen, Black Gnat. Early in the season use hooks No. 6 to 8; later, No. 8 to 12. Use the small patterns on streams, and the large patterns on lakes and rough waters; and, as I have repeatedly suggested, when the day is bright and where the water is clear, use the small flies of plain colors; on dark days and in the evening, use the large bright flies.

Dyed-Feather Flies.—"Some Anglers say no dyed feathers should be used in tying flies, that they fade to a damaging extent. We have always found dyed feathers practicable."—London Rod and Gun.

The Brown Hackle.—"Fasten red (crimson red) wool round a hook, and fit into the wool two feathers which grow under a cock's wattles."—Ælian, third century, A.D. "Out of the thousands of trout that I have caught, it is safe to say that over 70 per cent. were taken with the Brown Hackle."—C. T. Ramsey. Two hundred Anglers, representing all parts of the United States, contributed fly-fishing chapters to 137 Favorite Flies. Mary Orvis Marbury's wonderful volume on artificial flies and fly-fishing, and 130 of them declared the Brown Hackle their favorite pattern. "I had supposed that the Red Hackle was an imitation of the small red caterpillar, but the veteran Nessmuk affirms that it resembles nothing below or above. It is his favorite bug, and that settles the question."—H. C. Wilcox, Favorite Flies.

138

CHAPTER XXII

CASTING THE FLY

"Ah, tired man! Go find a spot
Somewhere in solitude;
Take hammock, books and tackle
And wearing apparel crude.

And live, if but the shortest time.
A wild life in the wood
A-fishing, reading, dreaming.
And you'll declare it good."
J. Milton Harkins.

Up and Down Stream.—English Anglers wade upstream, and some Anglers in America do the same. There is good reason in this manner of wading on the part of the old country's Anglers, because where they practice it the water is quiet and not altogether shallow. In America, where our trout waters are rapid and foaming as they rush along, it is not practical as a general rule to wade upstream. The walking is difficult, you become wet, the trout see you notwithstanding they lie face up stream, your flies drift toward you, it is hard to keep the line from being slack all the time, the flies sink too often, and altogether you spoil the chances of creeling whatever is takable in the stream. On still, barely-flowing, deep waters a line may be cast up or down stream.

Down Stream.—"There is much diversity of opinion about the manner of fishing, whether up or down the 139 stream. The great majority of Anglers, both in Europe and this country, favor the latter method, and very few the former."—John J. Brown.

Motion of the Fly.—In clear, smooth water let the fly sink a little; then move it along with a quick motion.

Manner in Fly-Fishing.—"The manner in which the flies are fished distinguishes the fly-fisherman from the mere fly-caster, whether or no the fly-caster, as such, be expert or otherwise."—Samuel G. Camp, The Fine Art of Fishing.

Fly-Casting Practice.—"When the learner becomes accustomed to handling his rod, he must try to perfect himself in two matters of great importance—accuracy and delicacy. Place a small piece of paper fifteen or twenty feet away, and aim at making the knot in the end of the line fall easily and quietly upon it. Your efforts will be aided if you will raise the point of the rod a trifle just as the forward impulse of the line is spent, and the line itself is straightened in the air for an instant in front. This is a novel kind of target shooting, but its usefulness will be realized when the Angler finds it necessary to drop his flies lightly just over the head of some wary trout."—Ripley Hitchcock.

The Magic Fly.—"Reader, did you ever throw the fly to tempt the silvery denizen of the lake or river to his destruction? Have you watched him, as it skimmed like a living insect along the surface, dart from his hiding-place and rush upon the tempting but deceitful morsel? Have you noticed his astonishment 140 when he found the hook was in his jaw? Have you watched him as he bent your slender rod 'like a reed shaken by the wind,' in his efforts to free himself, and then have you reeled him to your hand and deposited him in your basket as the spoil of your right arm? If you have not, leave the dull, monotonous, everyday things around you and try it."—S. S. Hammond.

Lifelike Fly.—Don't simply drag the fly through the water. Move your wrist gently up and down; then the lure will look and act like a living insect, not a bunch of hair or feather.

Nature-like Fly.—"In fly-fishing the lure must always be in motion." Excepting, say I, the instant when it first drops upon the pool. I have caught many of my largest trout—sometimes two at a single cast—the moment the fly touched the water.

Dry-Fly Success.—"There are no insurmountable obstacles in the way of becoming a successful dry-fly Angler that do not confront the user of the sunken fly."—Emlyn M. Gill, Practical Dry-Fly Fishing.

Correct Fly-Fishing Line.—"Nothing in reference to fly-fishing can be answered with such ease and confidence as the question what line should be used. Unquestionably the enameled waterproofed line, and no other."—Henry P. Wells.

Sunken Fly.—"Every bass fly-fisherman knows that to let his flies sink for a depth of six or eight inches is alluring. Under certain conditions, when after 141 trout, to let the flies descend for a depth of two feet before retrieving, is to tempt some sleepy old monster to attack. "—O. W. Smith.

The Strike.—"The moment the trout seizes the artificial fly, it is as far in his mouth as it ever will be; therefore, you cannot strike too quickly after you have seen or felt the trout."—D. W. Cross.

142

CHAPTER XXIII

TACKLE TALKS

"Slight lines of hair surprise the finny prey."
Pope.
"See that all things be right
For 'tis a very spite
To want tools, when a man goes afishing."
Charles Cotton.
To Extract Hooks.—Cut the snell free and push the hook on through, depressing the upper end so as to bring the point out as near as possible to where it went in. Don't try to pull the hook back.

Knots in Rodwood.—Don't switch a light rod sideways. The maker may have purposely put a knot to one side, and this would cause the rod to snap.

Function of the Rod.—"The essential and most important office of a rod is that which is exhibited after the fish is hooked ... in other words, in the playing and landing of the fish. In practical angling the act of casting, either with fly or bait, is preliminary and subordinate to the real uses of the rod. The poorest fly-rod made will cast a fly thirty or forty feet, which is about as far as called for in ordinary angling. But it is the continuous spring and yielding 143 resistance of the bent rod, constantly maintained, that not only tires out the fish, but protects the weak snell or leader from breakage, and prevents a weak hold of the hook from giving way; and this is the proper function of the rod."— James A. Henshall, Favorite Fish and Fishing.

Silkworm Gut.—"The features to be sought are good color, a hard, wiry texture, roundness, even diameter from end to end, and length. From these are to be inferred the strength and wearing quality of the gut, which are what we wish to estimate. From the color we infer whether the gut is fresh or stale, its probable strength in relation to its thickness, and, in part, its wearing quality. In all these respects fresh gut is superior to old gut of original equal quality. The color can best be judged from the fuzzy end of the hank, and should be clear and glassy, and by no means dull or yellowish. The wearing quality of the gut may be judged partly by its color, partly by its springiness when bent and released, and also by its hardness. It should feel like wire."—Henry P. Wells, Fly-Rods and Fly-Tackle.

Ronalds' Rod.—"The best materials are ash for the stock, lancewood for the middle, and bamboo for the tip."—Alfred Ronalds (1836).

South's Rod.—Theophilus South, in his Fly Fisher's Text Book (London, 1845), prefers ash to willow for butts, hickory for middle joints, and favors tips made from lancewood, cane, and whalebone, spliced together—four and even five pieces in a tip.

144

Lightest Rod.—Benjamin S. Whitehead fly-fishes with a gold-and-ivory-mounted split bamboo rod weighing one and eleven sixteenths ounces.

Tapered Line.—"The line for dry-fly fishing should be either single-tapered or double-tapered; the fine end of the taper will make more of an inconspicuous connection with the leader and with a tapered line casting ability is doubled."—Robert Page Lincoln.

Knife and Shears.—A small pair of scissors attached to a string and fastened to the Angler's coat are useful companions along the stream. They are more easily operated than a knife; they save time, and while you may do with them nearly all that can be done with a knife, they will render a service that cannot be obtained from the single blade. A knife should always be carried, nevertheless, and the proper one for the trout Angler is that newly invented thing which requires no finger-nail work and which is made ready for service by a mere pressure of the thumb on the top of the handle.

Trouting Outfit.—Here's a plain, practical, reasonable-price outfit with no unnecessary items: A four-ounce lancewood fly-rod, a common rubber click reel to hold twenty-five yards of fine waterproof silk line, a seventy-five cent cane landing-net, small and with no metal on it, a seventy-five cent creel, a dozen of the best made and highest-priced assorted trout-flies, a pair of waders, and a dollar's worth of the finest and best made silk gut leaders.

Rod Dressing.—To whip rings or guides on the rod use silk twist, drawing the final end through a few 145 coils of the whipping by means of a loose loop. To revarnish, wipe off all grease stains, and dress lightly down with the best copal. To reblacken brasses, mix a little lampblack with spirit varnish. Dress once or twice and let the dressing thoroughly dry before using the copal.

Buy your Tackle.—The old Anglers tied their flies themselves, and, in fact, made all their rods and tackle, save, perhaps, lines. To-day few Anglers think of tying flies or preparing any tackle, owing to the expertness and moderate terms on the part of dealers. It is much cheaper to buy tackle outright, as it is to buy gun shells ready loaded.

To Remove a Ferrule.—Hold it over the flame of a spirit lamp or any flame until the cement is softened. If it has been pinned on, take a large needle, break it off squarely, put it on the pin, and strike just hard enough to set the pin below the ferrule, then warm and remove.

The Joints.—If your rod joints go together harshly or do not come apart with ease, oil them lightly. See that no sand or any dirt gets in the ferrules. To take the joints apart easily when they are tightly set, gently warm the metal.

Rubber Bands.—Little rubber bands are practical items of a sportsman's outfit. One real service they render is in holding the fly-rod joints together when you travel through the woods after your day's fishing.

The Rod as a Measure.—"The size of a fish can be found out very easily, simply by having the butt of 146 the fishing rod marked off in inches up to two feet."—John Koltzan.

Position of the Reel.—The reel of a bait-rod should be on the top side of the rod, in front of the handle; that of a fly-rod, on the under side below the handle.

Cork Handle.—To avoid blisters on the hand, have the handle of your rod covered with cork instead of cane, twine, or rubber. It will prevent the hand from slipping, is pleasant to the touch, and very light in weight.

Smooth Ferrules.—Before jointing your rod, oil the male ferrules with vaseline, or by rubbing them on the back of your neck. This will prevent the joints from becoming tight after the day's sport.

Be Particular.—The finer the tackle the fairer the sport.

Care of the Rod.—See that your rod-case is thoroughly dry before you put your rod in it, and always tie the case-strings loosely or you will have bent tips and joints.

Tackle Tells.—"The quality of gameness in a fish is best determined by the character of the tackle used. A brook trout on a striped bass rod, or a black bass on a tarpon rod, could not, in either case, exhibit its characteristic gameness, or afford any sport to the Angler. Excellent sport with small fishes, however, is now rendered possible owing to the advent of the very light trout rod. It should not be considered beneath the dignity of an Angler to cast the fly for a rock bass, a blue-gill, or a croppie, with a three-ounce rod. Certainly 147 it is just as sportsmanlike as to fish for six-inch brook trout in a meadow brook or a mountain rill."—James A. Henshall.

76

Rust Preventive.—Use animal oil free of salt on any metal—steel, iron, brass, German silver, etc. Vaseline may be used on brass and German silver; mercurial ointment on steel and iron. Don't use ordinary vegetable oil.

Telescopic Reel.—An English reel, the telescope winch, can be expanded to carry a double quantity of line or less at will. By its means a trout reel becomes a salmon reel or bass reel or vice versa as you please.

Fine Tackle.—"His tackle for bricht, airless days is o' gossamere; and at a wee distance aff you think he's fishin' without ony line ava."—The Ettrick Shepherd.

Dressing for Silk Wrappings.—Cobbler's wax dissolved in spirits of wine. Paint it on with a feather.

Line Dressing.—Deer's fat solidifies at a higher temperature than most fats and will cling well.

Black Leader and Snell.—"For trout, use a black leader and have your hooks snelled with black gut."—"Country Pumpkin."

Thin Line.—"The thinner the line I use the more fish I catch."—A. Hamilton, Jr.

Cocoon Lines.—The Japanese now make almost invisible fishing lines from cocoons. The silk threads are boiled in oil and glue and calendered under heavy 148 pressure. The fish cannot see these lines, and they are effective against the gamest species.

Enameled Line.—"In casting from the reel I use a soft silk line, but I prefer to strip cast. In strip casting it is absolutely necessary to use a good enameled line. The reason I prefer strip casting is that a long, slender rod can be used. No other line than an enameled one can be stripped into the bottom of the boat and permitted to run out rapidly without snarling."—"Greenhorn."

Making a Camp Rod.—Surgeon's plaster, in tin spools, or electrician's adhesive tape, are serviceable in many ways in camp. You can even build a makeshift casting rod if you've forgotten or lost the real article. Fasten the reel to a stiff section of any fishing rod or a straight light-weight tree switch with the tape. Screw eyes or small staples will answer for the running guides, but finer guides and a cleaner-looking tip guide may be made with fine wire and the tape.

Tackle and Time.—Correct fishing tackle is as necessary in the hands of the tyro as with the practical Angler, but the beginner mustn't expect tackle, however appropriate, to be all that is required to make toward perfection in angling; experience and practice are equally important. As an apprentice in carpentry who may have all the tools of his master still needs experience and actual practice, so the young Angler fully equipped with good tackle must serve an apprenticeship on the waters.

CHAPTER XXIV

THE ANGLER'S KITCHEN

"The reputation that trout enjoy as a food-fish is partly due to the fact that they are usually cooked over an open fire.... The real reason why food cooked over an open fire tastes so good to us is because we are really hungry when we get it."—Henry van Dyke.

"Moses, the friend of God—Lev. xi., 9, Deut. xiv., 9,—appointed fish to be the chief diet for the best commonwealth that ever yet was. The mightiest feasts have been of fish."—Walton.

"... and fish the last
Food was that He on earth did taste."
W. Basse.
"If you eat your kind, we will eat you."—Benj. Franklin.

Catching vs. Cooking.—"I care little whether I catch a fish on a No. 6 or a No. 5 hook, or whether I use a $3 reel or a $2.99 one. Whether I use bay leaves, or cloves, or mushrooms, or tomato sauce, or tartar sauce in preparing my fish is more important. Game is improved by hanging for a while, but fish should be eaten as soon as possible after being caught."—"Piscator."

Fish as Food.—The great variety of flavors in fish food makes an ichthyological diet more palatable than 150 quadruped meat, and therefore more healthful because only that which is eaten with a relish is digestible and nourishing.

Forest Fish Sauce.—Use a wild rose berry to make a sauce for fish food in camp.

Carp.—The carp, celebrated in ancient song and story as the meat of kings, is as savory as the trout or any other fish species if cooked and served correctly.

Preserving Fish.—Don't pack fish in wet grass or anything damp. Use dry straw.

Frozen Fish.—Don't freeze fish unless you keep it frozen until quite ready for the fire, as it spoils soon after thawing.

Scaling Fish.—Use an ordinary horse currycomb.

CHAPTER XXV

"The water, more productive than the earth, Nature's store-house, in which she locks up her wonders, is the eldest daughter of the creation, the element upon which the spirit of God did first move."—Izaak Walton.

Transporting Trout.—To bring your fish home, first clean them carefully, taking pains to remove that little dark blood streak along the backbone. Then, after wiping them dry, pack them in ferns, separately, and free from ice. Never send your fish home by express; take them with you. A box cannot be checked on the train. Use an old packing trunk. In this you can also transport your heavy outfit—wading boots, oilskins, landing-net, etc.

Trout in Captivity.—Trout in artificial ponds should be fed three or four times a week in the winter time during the very warmest part of the day. There is no natural food in artificial ponds, and feeding is necessary in order to keep the big fish from eating their small companions. In natural trout ponds fed by springs so much care need not be exercised in winter. Air holes need not be cut in any ice that may form, as the springs afford a proper temperature, and but little food, if any, need be given the fish.

152

Killing the Trout.—Kill your trout the instant they are landed; don't let them suffer slow death. The game deserves humane treatment, and the meat tastes better by quick killing.

Trout Destroyers.—Eels are ruinous to trout. They eat trout spawn, and they should be removed from all trout waters.

Live Frozen Trout.—Trout packed in ice for several days and carried forty miles by stagecoach and two hundred and fifty miles by railway (Feb., 1914) from the State of Washington to Montana, says the Lewiston Democrat of Butte, Montana, came to life and swam spryly when placed in a tank of water at the end of their journey—Hennessy's meat store at Butte.

Water Plants.—Aquatic plants, besides affording protection and shade to the fishes, supply oxygen to the water.

Growth of Trout.—"Mr. Tomkin of Polgaron put some small river trout, 2-1/2 inches in length, into a newly made pond. He took some of them out the second year, above twelve inches in length; the third year, he took one out of sixteen inches in length; and the fourth year, one of twenty-five inches in length: this was in 1734."—Carew's Survey of Cornwall.

Ducks Eat Trout.—Arthur A. Woodford and S. W. Eddy, of Avon, Conn., say that ducks eat trout and destroy the trout's breeding places by digging in the banks along the ponds and streams.

CHAPTER XXVI

THE ANGLER'S CLOTHING AND FOOTWEAR

And let your garments russet be or gray.
Of colour darke, and hardest to descry.
Pleasures of Angling.

Hobnail Footwear.—Most any boot or shoe can be used for wading the trout streams, but a special selection is always best for every sort of purpose. Rubber, canvas, and leather are employed in the making of the fisherman's footwear. The hobnail heel-and-sole pattern is the correct article for use in swift-running water. The hobnail recommended above all others is the common, cheap soft-iron hobnail with corrugated head; carry a package in your tackle box.

Repairing Waders.—Patch holes in rubber boots and rubber stockings, etc., by covering the holes with thin sheet rubber, cementing this with a mixture of black rubber dissolved in spirits of turpentine.

Drying Rubber Boots.—Fill 'em full of hot bran.

Clothing.—Sack coats, heavy trousers, a stout vest, all with plenty of large pockets. In color the garments should be gray, drab, or brown.

Hat.—A soft felt of gray shade.

Boots and Shoes.—Brown leather.

Waders.—Leather shoes with holes in the sides or canvas shoes for summer. Rubber boots or wading trousers for cold weather.

Woolen and Rubber Clothing.—Good quality woolen will shed rain for hours. Wear rubber outer garments in a wet brushy trail.

CHAPTER XXVII

LITTLE CASTS

The Fingerling Fisher.—It is sad to see a man with his creel full of trout each not over the size of a lady's penknife. This character has a photograph made of himself with the fingerlings held in front of him so as to make them appear of legal size; this he sends to friends in the city with glowing accounts of his catch of "a hundred speckled beauties in one day."

Tent Waterproofing.—Sugar of lead and alum.

Woodcraft.—A good, simple way to find a road or dwelling, if you are lost in the woods, is to follow down a stream.

Destroying the Streams.—Discourage the indiscriminate cutting down of trees. The destruction of forest land means the drying up of trout waters and the waste of drinking water.

The Bungler.—Bragging of ungentle catches, untruths about the size of a specimen, and non-ichthyological nonsense about the mystery of a species—unnatural history such as cheap fiction writers indulge in—by bungling would-be fishermen annoy the practical man and puzzle the earnest tyro. The record of honest sport is entertaining and instructive.

156

Discrimination.—Do not worry if the fish are small so long as they are of legal size; reduce your tackle. A vest-pocket watch keeps just as good time as a town-hall clock.

Sportsmanship.—Chivalry to his companion and humane treatment to the game he pursues are the Angler's axioms.

Giving Fishes to Neighbors.—Don't give your neighbors part of your catch. They won't appreciate it. They'll throw them away in most cases. If they cook and eat them they suffer the belief that they are doing you a favor. Most recipients of fishes think the specimens too small, or that they have too many bones, or that they are too thin, too tough, too hard to scale, etc. They'd rather have a bought-and-paid-for cold-storage cod of ten pounds than a freshly caught brook trout presented by an Angler friend.

Not All of Fishing to Fish.—"The fisherman whose catching of many fish causes him to forget his surroundings, blinds his eyes to the beauties of Nature, and deadens his ears to the music of the wild, is no Angler."—O. W. Smith.

157

CHAPTER XXVIII

BORROWED LINES

"Oh I could wish the lord to say
That all the twelve months
Should be May."
George Borrow.
"I borrow no man's tackle."—"Frank Forester."

Nature.—"Solitude has its charm and its reward and Nature offers to mankind the proper blessings, be they indulged in with care and consideration. The mind that has been oppressed by following civilization's rut will find ample comfort in the solitude given man by Nature."—R. P. L., The Sportsmen's Review.

Save the Fishes.—"We who love wild life and long ago abandoned the many instruments of extermination and who have come to a more considerate mode of recreation should do all in our power to discourage its destruction and to encourage the propagation of the wild life which has been so generously and graciously given us by our Creator. Only extremists insist on terrible slaughter of fishes, birds, and quadrupeds."—E. M. Hermann.

"Improvement."—"No building enterprise, no 'betterment' ever spares a tree. Insects and lack of 158 care kill what 'improvement' leaves."—New York Evening World, Aug. 18, 1914.

Jesus the Fisherman.—"Had not the Saviour of Gennesaret understood fishermen's signs, such as the riff on the water, the schooling of the fishes, the hovering gulls, there would have been no miraculous catch of fishes."—Charles Hallock.

Society where None Intrudes.—"I had pined so much, in the dust and heat of the great town, for trees and fields, and running waters, and the sounds of country life, and the air of country winds, that never more could I grow weary of these soft enjoyments."—Blackmore, Lorna Doone.

The Call of the Wild.—"Lying hidden away in the back of the brain is the primitive longing for adventure and the tingle of the nerves that awaits it. Under the veneer of what is called civilization lie the racial and elemental passions, just as Mother Earth lies beneath the asphalted streets of the city."—Adele M. Ballard.

Gold Fishing.—"When all green places have been destroyed in the builder's lust of gain; when all the lands are but bricks and piles of wood and iron; when there is no moisture anywhere and no rain ever falls; when the sky is a vault of smoke and all the rivers reek with poison; when forest and stream, the moor and meadow and all the old green wayside beauty are things vanished and forgotten; when every gentle, timid thing of brake and bush, of air and water, has been killed because it robbed them of a berry or a 159 fruit; when the earth is one vast city, whose young children behold neither the green of the field nor the blue of the sky, and hear no song but the hiss of the steam, and know no music but the roar of the furnace; when the old sweet silence of the countryside, and the old sweet sounds of waking birds, and the old sweet fall of summer showers, and the grace of a hedgerow bough, and the glow of the purple heather, and the note of the cuckoo and cushat, and the freedom of waste and of woodland and all things are dead and remembered of no man; then the world, like the Eastern king, will perish miserably of famine and of drought, with gold in its stiffened hands, and gold in its withered lips and gold everywhere; gold that the people can neither eat nor drink, gold that cares nothing for them, but mocks them horribly; gold for which their fathers sold peace, and health, and holiness, and beauty; gold that is one vast grave."—Ouida.

Heaven.—"My heart is fixed firm and stable in the belief that ultimately the sunshine and the summer, the flowers and the azure sky, shall become, as it were, interwoven into man's existence. He shall take from all their beauty and enjoy their glory."—Richard Jefferies, The Life of the Fields.

Modern Savagery.—"Civilization is a nervous disease."—Clarence King.

Humanity.—"Reading and writing are not educational, unless they make us feel kindly towards all creatures."—Ruskin.

Walton's Depth.—"In Walton's angling works a child may wade and a giant swim."—John Ryan.

161

"I shall stay ... [the reader no longer than to wish him a rainy evening to read this ... Discourse; and that, if he be an honest Angler, the East wind may never blow when he goes a-Fishing."—Izaak Walton, The Compleat Angler, 1653.

APPRECIATIONS:

"Princeton, May 30, 1900—"The
Determined Angler ... the
most pleasantly written, the
most sensible and practical and
instructive volume I have ever
seen of its kind."
Cleveland signature
The Art Of Angling.— ... a
book on the art of angling,
with a hearty indorsement from
the most famous of latter-day
fishermen, former President
Grover Cleveland. It fully
deserves this indorsement.—New
York Herald, September 22,

1900.

The Trout And The Whale.
— ... rare sympathy and
genuine knowledge. Mr. Bradford
undoubtedly knows, as
did his sainted forerunner, that
"there are fish, as namely the
whale, three times as big as the
mighty elephant, that is so fierce
in battle," yet a single salve-liner
fontinalis of "just a little
over two pounds and a quarter"
is the single luxury he allows
himself. Mr. Bradford's dealings
are with those sophisticated
denizens of much-fished streams,
that have to be approached with
the finesse of a diplomat and
handled with the swift skill of a
fencing master. In all that
pertains to this difficult and
studious art one feels that Mr.
Bradford is an adept, and that the
graceful, commendatory letter
from former President Cleveland
is amply merited.—New York
Evening Telegram, September
8, 1900.

Practical.—Practical advice.
—New York Sun.

Angling Converts.—There
is always a real charm about
what is written on the subject of
fishing, by real disciples of old
Izaak Walton, and the reason
may be found in the fact that
the spirit of the greatest of
anglers has come upon them.
The Determined Angler is no
exception to the rule. It is
good reading, full of wisdom and
instruction. And while it will
prove very useful to the beginner
and even the veteran, it is also
calculated to make many converts

to the rod and line. The
book is full of wise counsel and
information.—New York Evening
Sun, September 8, 1900.

For Fair Fishermen.—Appeals
to those who fish fair.... Charles
Bradford, the
modern American authority on
angling.—New York Press.

For Gentle Readers.—Much
good advice and very
pleasant entertainment for any
gentle reader.—New York Observer.

Summer And Winter.—Pleasant
reading whether by the
winter fireside or the shaded
banks of summer.—New York
Evening Post.

Angling Experience.—Mr.
Bradford is no novice in this line
of literature.—New York Athletic
Club Journal.

Angling Philosophy.—Breathes
the very essence of
philosophy; the result of much
experience.—Brooklyn (N. Y.)
Eagle.

Waltonian Spirit.—Pervaded
by the spirit of Izaak
Walton.—The Outlook.

The Gentle Trout.—The
author is an enthusiastic devotee
of the sport [angling, upon
which he writes with a contagious
enthusiasm ... an angler
of very positive convictions; he
has a fixed aversion to fishing
with the scarlet ibis, and confesses
to a personal preference
to sober colors in flies for all
seasons and on all waters. Above

all, he insists upon the use of
the most scientific methods,
since "a trout is a gentleman,
and should be treated as such
and lured with only delicate and
humane weapons." A facsimile
of a letter of warm commendation
from ex-President
Cleveland serves as frontispiece
to this agreeable volume which
is attractively printed.—New
York Commercial Advertiser.
September 13, 1900.

The Gentle Art.—A gentle
exponent of a gentle art.—Denver
(Colo.) Republican.

APPRECIATIONS:

Wild Brook Trout.—The
announcement of a new book
on fishing interests a class of the
community, especially those
confined to the cities, which is
increasing year by year. This
work depicts a trout fisherman's
paradise. It is from the same
graphic pen as The Wildfowlers,
and divulges many a secret of
the fisherman's craft. One may
learn from its pages where a
gentle creel of real wild brook
trout may be made in a morning's
pleasant angling, "in a
free and comparatively virgin
gameland—a wild and naturally
beautiful country, embracing
all the charms of scenic splendor
for which the American brook
trout regions are famous," and
its pages contain an abundance
of practical detail concerning
tackle and methods of casting
the fly, and playing and landing
the game ... it makes a notable

addition to the sportsman's library.—New York Home Journal, May 10, 1900.

The Angler's Art.—Mr. Bradford gives eminently practical hints on the angler's art.—Salt Lake City (Utah) Telegram.

A Study Of Fishing.—The advice comes from one who has learned many things about fishing.—Utica (N. Y.) Press.

Comprehensive Angling.—One of the most comprehensive bits of angling literature we have had for many a long year, and thoroughly deserves the generous praise it has received ... the most delightful fishing book of this generation—The Amateur Sportsman.

The Angler's Library.—deserves a place in the library of every fly-fisherman.—The Sportsman's Magazine.

A Fisher Of Men.—Mr. Bradford may well be proud of this tribute, for Mr. Cleveland is himself a determined angler and an experienced fisher of men.—Spirit of the Times.

Secrets Of The Fish.—What he has to tell of the secrets known only to the fish, himself, and a few others is marvelous.—Montreal (Canada) Gazette.

Philosophy And Fishing.—With this kind of man philosophy and fishing mix well.—Rochester (N. Y.) Herald.

Quality, Not Quantity.—Mr.
Bradford writes for those
who see more in the trip than
the frying-pan.—Savannah (Ga.)
News.

Walton's Follower.—A
true disciple of Izaak Walton.—
London (Eng.) Post.

Angling Enthusiasm.—An
accomplished and enthusiastic
angler.—Cincinnati (Ohio) Star.

Cleveland's Words.—Charles
Bradford writes practical and
sensible books.—Philadelphia
(Pa.) Public Ledger.

Angling Anticipations.—Mr.
Bradford believes fishing is
a means and not an end.—Albany
Argus.

Joyous Material.—He has
gathered material to make the
heart of the fisherman leap for
joy.—Boston Transcript.

Would Please Walton.—Izaak
Walton, Christopher
North, and the other mighty
fishermen known to fame, would
wag their wise heads approvingly
over Mr. Bradford's book.
The Pilgrims who told King
James that they desired to go
God and catch fishes would
accord Mr. Bradford's volume
a place beside the Bay Psalm
Book.—Pittsburg (Pa.) Gazette.

Entertaining.—Mr. Bradford
has written before on angling,
and very entertainingly.—Saturday
Evening Post (Phila.).

Contemplative Man.—Charles
Bradford is one to

whom, as Washington Irving said, "There is something in angling that tends to produce a gentleness of spirit and a pure serenity of mind."—Dundee (Scot.) Adv.

Universal Reading.—The descriptive matter is both interesting and instructive. Fishermen in all parts of the country will find the book well worth reading.—Bay City (Mich.) Tribune, July 19, 1900.